HONOR BRIGHT

HONOR BRIGHT

A Play in Two Acts

by

LUE MORGAN DOUTHIT

THE COBHAM AND HATHERTON PRESS
Cleveland, Ohio
1988

Book design by Roderick Boyd Porter

Library of Congress Cataloging-in-Publication Data

Douthit, Lue Morgan, 1957-
Honor bright: a play in two acts / by Lue Morgan Douthit.
— first edition

p. cm.
ISBN 0-944125-03-4
I. Title.
PS3554.0875H6 1988
812'.54—dc19 87-28096
CIP

FOR HAL AND MARY

FOREWORD

Honor Bright was presented at the McGinn/Cazale Theatre by Crossroads Theatre Productions during October 16-27, 1984. It was produced by Diane Wicks and directed by Bruce Levitt. Scenery was by Mike Boak, lighting by Greg MacPherson, and costumes by John Deering. The production stage manager was Nan Siegmund, the stage manager, Maude Brickner, and assistant director, Pia Haas. In order of speaking the cast was: Sharon Hope (Sarah), Leslie Lachlan (Mrs. Barnett), Robert Trumbull (Mr. Barnett), Jane Gabbert-Wilson ("Edie"), Jennifer Kaiser (Young Edie Barnett), Siri Wannamaker (Janet Townsend), Tom McBride (Jessie Adams), Dana Delany (Edie Barnett), Richard Duggan (Chip Barnett), and Karen Braga (Kate Barnett).

CAST OF CHARACTERS

YOUNG EDIE BARNETT . . . . . the adolescent version of Edie, age sixteen to twenty-two years

EDIE BARNETT . . . . Edie as she was in the present, age twenty-two to twenty-four years

"EDIE" . . . . . . as she appears to us now, a typical preppie

JESSIE . . . . Edie's boyfriend

CHARLES BARNETT . . . . Edie's father

MARIAN BARNETT . . . . Edie's mother

CHIP BARNETT . . . . Edie's brother

KATHERINE BARNETT . . . . Edie's sister

JANET TOWNSEND . . . . Edie's best friend

SARAH . . . . the Barnett's maid

ACT ONE

ACT ONE

SCENE: (The stage is split into two levels; one on top of the other. The top level represents a one bedroom apartment in Boston with a living room area, a kitchen area, and a hall leading to the bedroom and bathroom which are both offstage. The lower level is the living room of a rather large house, upper-middle-class in nature, suburban in content. There is a sunken living room with a baby grand piano and a bar. A foyer is upstage and there is a staircase leading up to rooms which we do not see. We see the front door off to one side of the foyer; the kitchen is off to the other side.)

TIME: (The present; an early evening in February.)

AT RISE: (Mr. and Mrs. Barnett are sitting in the living room downstairs at an approximate forty-five degree angle to each other, facing the audience. The lights remain dark on the apartment upstairs.)

(Long pause. Charles *is sipping a martini,* Marian *a scotch.* Charles *is a fifty-five-year-old successful lawyer. He has a look about him that says he came from money — intelligent, generous, yet knows his station in life. He expects what he has. It is not really arrogance; it is, for him, fact.* Marian *is his fifty-three-year-old wife. Junior League, tennis, fund-raising chairman for the American Cancer Association, alumni trustee for her alma mater — very social, very intelligent, very beautiful. They*

remain sitting and sipping for some time, never looking at one another, lost in thought. Occasionally, Charles *will pick up a magazine and try to concentrate, but it is obvious that his mind is elsewhere.* Marian *does not even pretend to be with us. She continues to have a quizzical, almost glazed look on her face.)*

(Phone begins to ring. There is a telephone extension in the living room on the desk, but neither of them reacts to it. Charles *looks offstage in the direction of the kitchen. Then he returns to his drink. The phone stops ringing after six or seven rings.)*

(Several more beats pass. Enter Sarah *from upstage, where we might suppose the kitchen would be. She cautiously crosses into the living room. She is a middle-aged woman, somewhat heavy set. She has been with the Barnetts for so long that she has become almost indispensable. She has helped raise the children and run the household. She has become more than the maid. She is definitely one of the family; yet, still in the old style, she knows her place.)*

SARAH

Mrs. B . . . . ?

(No response. Sarah *moves in closer.)*

Mrs. B . . . . ?

MARIAN

(Startled by the interruption)

Hm?

(Shakes herself)

Yes, Sarah . . . ?

SARAH

I hope you don't mind, but the phone was ringing for such a long . . .

Charles

It was fine, Sarah. Thanks for answering it.

Sarah

(Nods her head in acknowledgment)

Mrs. B, about . . .

Marian

Not now, Sarah, can't the phone message wait?

Sarah

Of course, ma'am, but what I really wanted to know was when you and Mr. B were planning on eating supper.

Marian

Oh.

Sarah

You should eat something.

*(*Marian *has lapsed back into her "trance.")*

Charles

(Jumping in)

Sarah, why don't you put together some sandwiches or whatever and leave them on the sideboard. We'll get to them when we get hungry, o.k.?

Sarah

Yes, sir, fine.

(She exits.)

Charles

Marian . . . ?

Marian

Charles, I'm really not hungry.

Charles

I know, but Sarah feels so useless lately. She's not sure how to help.

MARIAN

Please, dear, don't.

*(*Charles *finishes his drink.)*

CHARLES

I'm going for a refill. Want one?

MARIAN

Yes.

(She finishes her drink and hands him the glass.)

CHARLES

Have you heard from Kate today?

(He crosses to the bar and mixes the drinks.)

MARIAN

She called twice, as a matter of fact.

CHARLES

Ah, and how is she?

MARIAN

She's fine. She wanted to know how I was.

CHARLES

(Crosses to Marian *with both drinks)*

Ah, and how are you?

MARIAN

(Takes her drink from Charles*)*

Fine. How are you?

*(*Charles *begins to answer, but sees that* Marian *has looked away. He shrugs and crosses to his chair. Both sit and sip, not looking at each other, as the lights slowly dim on their scene.)*

(Spotlight comes up on "Edie," *who is located between the upper and lower levels. This place, throughout the play, will be her "place." She is sitting as the light hits her. She is twenty-three, thin, but of an athletic build, average height. She*

is very pretty, in that innocent WASPish way. There is a certain intelligence about her that you wouldn't expect — perhaps because you can't see it right away; it's there, it's just hard to see. "Edie" *can move around, joining in with other action, but she can neither talk with characters nor change the course of the action, no matter how much she may want to.)*

(The phone upstairs begins to ring as the lights begin a slow fade up on apartment.)

"EDIE"

Those are my parents, Mr. and Mrs. Charles Robert Barnett, the Fifth, if you want to be exact. They've been like that for almost two weeks now.

(The phone has been answered by one of those answering machines. We hear the messages.)

("Hey, it's me. Your parents just called me. They can't seem to get in touch with you. Call them, please?")

You see, two weeks ago, I didn't decide to just move out of my parents' lives. I decided to move out of my own as well.

("Edith . . . ")

("Edie" *winces.)*

("Edith, your father and I have been trying to reach you for two days. Please call home.")

I mean, I am twenty-three years old and I decided to make some decisions on my own, without them, without anybody. Is that so terrible?

("Edie, it's me again. Are you all right? Call me, o.k.?")

(A pounding begins on the door outside the upstairs apartment. Someone is banging a fist against the door.)

(The banging continues upstairs, followed by Jessie's *voice. "Edie, hey Edieee . . . Edith, I know*

you're in there . . . ")

It was the first time in my life that I decided to do something on my own, about my life, which I felt and still feel was the act of a rational, intelligent woman.

(By now, Jessie *has put his shoulder to the door and has opened it. He looks around, yells "Edieee" one time and heads for the bathroom door, which is slightly ajar.)*

(We hear Jessie *moan from the bathroom.)*

*(*Jessie *says "Oh, my God" several times, overlapping* "Edie"*'s next few lines.)*

I mean, can't you see that when you start at such a high level in life, there's nowhere to go? I saw it as two choices: either you stay the same, or you regress — neither choice made me very happy. You know what my father used to say about me?

(Lights upstairs begin to fade as they come up on Marian *and* Charles *in living room.* Charles *has a letter in his hand.)*

CHARLES

Did you read this letter from Edie? I think she's depressed. She should exercise.

"EDIE"

That's not exactly what I had in mind.

CHARLES

That poor child. She's never going to be happy until she accepts who she is and learns to live with it.

(Lights out.)

"EDIE"

My poor father. I always felt sorry for him because I felt that's exactly what he did — learned to live with it. Don't get me wrong — I don't hate my family. They may be thinking that, but it's not true. Out of everything I may say, you have to believe that. Right now, though, I'm just not exactly sure what they do think. I know that they're confused. But, you see, I'm not. I know what happened and I know why it happened. They probably even think that it's their fault. But it isn't. It was my choice. I want to show you what I remember, as I remember it, to prove once and for all what is the truth — my version of my story.

(As "Edie" *begins the introductions, the lights will come up downstairs to segue into the next scene.)*

You already know my mother and father, Wheaton '52 and Brown '50, respectively. And, of course, you know Sarah, who's been with us ever since she and I can remember.

(Lights up reveal Charles *and* Marian *sitting.* Sarah *is serving them drinks.)*

Daddy's great-grandfather was a contemporary and colleague of Alexander Graham Bell, and was in at the beginning of what we now refer to as "Ma Bell." Money, as you may well imagine, has never been a problem — well, at least we never had to worry about paying our phone bills. Mother's side wasn't too shabby, either. Her grandfather was an original partner of Compton and Barrett, Esquires — a very big, prestigious law firm, very big.

(Phone begins to ring downstairs.)

That will no doubt be for me. Let me introduce myself. I am Edith Barrett Barnett. "Barrett Barnett" you say? I know. Barrett is my mother's maiden name. They say she almost didn't marry my father because the names were so much alike.

*(*Young Edie *comes racing down the stairs to answer the phone. She is followed by* Janet Townsend. *Both are wearing athletic tunics, with bloomers, tennis shoes, and are carrying field hockey sticks.* Young Edie's *hair is pulled back into a ponytail. She is a younger version of* "Edie." Janet *is a shorter, chunkier, sloppier version of* Young Edie. *She wears glasses, and her hair, although it, too, is pulled back, has several strands that have loosened down from the headband. Her glasses almost always are down on her nose.)*

That's Janet Townsend. Oh, my, I haven't thought about us like that for a long time. We were inseparable in high school. You know, the buddies-for-life routine.

YOUNG EDIE

She said that? That bitch.

CHARLES

Edie.

YOUNG EDIE

Sorry, Daddy.

*(*Young Edie *turns her attention to the phone, while* Janet *is trying to hear what is being said.* Young Edie *is constantly waving her off.)*

I don't believe it.

JANET

What?

YOUNG EDIE

Well, I don't care. Who died and made her head of the school anyway?

JANET

Who?

YOUNG EDIE

She's just jealous because I have Jessie . . .

MARIAN

Edith.

(Both "Edie" *and* Young Edie *wince.)*

"EDIE"

God, I hated it when she called me Edith.

MARIAN

Edith, you get off that phone this instant. Surely the two of you have something better to do — like your homework?

YOUNG EDIE

(Sighs heavily)

Yes, ma'am. Listen, Susie, I've got to go now. My mother needs me for something. I'll talk to you later, o.k.? Bye-bye.

JANET

What? What?

CHARLES

Edie, do you think that the two of you could continue that upstairs?

"EDIE"

A patient man, my father.

JANET

Tell me.

YOUNG EDIE

Well, Susie found out that Lillian talked to the headmistress today and now she thinks she has the power to give out more dress code violations and Susie thinks that it depends on how Lillian feels about you, you know, whether she likes you or not . . .

(Both begin to cross upstairs.)

JANET

You're kidding. That bitch.

YOUNG EDIE

Janet.

JANET

Sorry, Ede.

(Lights fade out downstairs, leaving a special on Marian *and* Charles *sitting and sipping. These lights will fade slowly and dissolve as lights begin to fade up on apartment. We see* Jessie *again. This time he is yelling through the bathroom door. It appears to be early morning.)*

JESSIE

Edie, are you all right in there? What's going on?

EDIE

I'm fine . . . now.

JESSIE

What is that? "I'm fine now?" Don't be so melodramatic.

"EDIE"

There were times when I didn't know how to be anything else.

EDIE

Calm down, egghead. I just threw up again. Wanna kiss me?

*(*Edie *comes out of the bathroom, looking the worse for wear, as if she has had a long bout with a bottle, which she indeed has. She is in age and appearance a cross between the other Edies. It is important that the three women playing* Edie *look alike — not as triplets, per se, but there should be enough resemblance to differentiate them in age, not in person.)*

JESSIE

Lord, no. I don't know how you managed to drink all that gin. I don't see how you're still alive.

"EDIE"

Well, if that's what he called living . . .

EDIE

This ain't exactly what I call living. You're supposed to be the doctor. Surely you understand the principle of "pickling."

(Laughs)

"EDIE"

That's me in my mature period.

JESSIE

Good God, you're still drunk. You know, Edie, sometimes, I don't even know who you are.

*(*Edie *crosses into the living room and passes out on the couch.* Jessie *goes to the kitchen and begins to make coffee.)*

"EDIE"

Flo Nightingale there in the kitchen is the only love in my life. What did I tell you about being melodramatic? Jessie is . . . was? . . . well, Jessie is a good person. He cared a lot about everything, including me. I wish now that . . . I guess . . .

EDIE

Did you call the lab for me?

JESSIE

Yes.

EDIE

What did you tell them?

JESSIE

The truth.

EDIE

Jessie.

JESSIE

(In a teasing tone)

I said that this was Dr. Adams calling and that I would send a note with little Edie tomorrow explaining why she didn't show up for work.

EDIE

Jessie.

JESSIE

Don't worry. It's all cool.

*(*Jessie *comes over to* Edie *and hands her a cup of coffee.)*

EDIE

I love you, dufus.

JESSIE

I know, pumpkin.

EDIE

I'll never hurt you, you know that, don't you?

JESSIE

Yes.

EDIE

Honor bright.

"EDIE"

Yes, but . . . I . . . never mind.

JESSIE

Why did you do it?

"EDIE" AND EDIE

Do what?

JESSIE

Drink that whole fucking bottle of gin? You could have died, you know.

"EDIE"

Always the doctor.

EDIE

I was thirsty?

JESSIE

God, you've been weird lately.

(He starts to get up, as if to leave.)

EDIE

Don't go now.

JESSIE

I have to. I have a class in a couple of hours that I need to review for.

"Edie"

Jessie was in medical school — Harvard, of course. Sometimes, however, that fact was exceedingly boring.

Edie

O.k., leave me to die, I don't care.

Jessie

(Takes this in stride)

Right. I hate to say it, but I think you're going to live. Yes, not only will you regain your balance and the use of your extremities, but you will also live to tell the tale. Take a couple of vitamin B tablets. Actually, a Bloody Mary might do you more good.

Edie

You have got to be kidding.

"Edie" and Jessie

A little hair of the dog?

Jessie

(He tousles her hair and heads for the door.)

I've got to go, Edie. Really. See you after class.

(He exits.)

*(*Edie *shakes her head and then looks as if she is about to be sick again. She races back to the bathroom as the lights fade down on the apartment, and slowly begin to fade up on the living room. As lights come up downstairs, we see* Chip *and* Kate *sitting in the living room.* Chip, *a very "Joe College" type, is eating an apple with his legs draped over a chair.* Katherine *is sitting at the desk, reading. She is a slim, long-haired, serious-looking girl with glasses, wearing a plaid skirt, monogrammed sweater, and penny loafers. As she begins to describe these two,* "Edie" *will enter the living room.)*

"EDIE"

The last two characters. The older brother, Chip. His real name, of course, is Charles Robert Barnett, the Sixth, but nobody ever called him that. He was always Chip, as in "chip off the old block." He's six years older than I am. Brown, of course.

(She crosses to her sister.)

The older sister, Katherine, or Kate to everyone except my mother. She is the intellectual of the family. Right now I think she is studying seventeenth-century sacred music. Four years older, an accomplished musician, and Wheaton. I am, er, was the baby, and as it turned out, Daddy's little girl. To say I was rebellious, I think, is an understatement.

*(*Young Edie *enters with a slam of the front door, rushing quickly upstairs discarding her school blazer as she goes, leaving it on the landing, while fumbling with the hooks and zipper of her school skirt. The phone begins to ring.)*

CHIP

My God, what was that? Edie?

"EDIE"

Of course.

YOUNG EDIE

(Shouting from upstairs)

Would somebody answer the phone, please? I'm expecting an important call.

CHIP

I bet. Probably that Jessie Adams again.

(He deliberately shuts his magazine and crosses to the desk. As he arrives, Kate, *who has answered it, hands the receiver to him, without missing a line in her book.)*

CHIP

Thanks.

KATE

Don't mention it.

CHIP

Hello.

KATE

(Shouting upstairs)

Edie. It's Janet.

CHIP

Yes, she is. Who may I say is calling?

KATE

She'll just be a minute.

(She listens to hear when Edie picks up the extension upstairs.)

CHIP

I don't understand her hurry to turn this place into a tornado every afternoon.

KATE

I think she probably just wants to take off that uniform.

(She hears that Edie has gotten the phone and hangs up.)

CHIP

What's with that uniform hatred? I had to wear a coat and tie every day to school. I never minded it.

"EDIE"

My brother could never quite grasp the real significance of things.

KATE

You probably would if it were blue — always and forever blue.

CHIP

I like blue.

KATE

You would.

"EDIE"

He would.

(Enter Young Edie *down the stairs, not wearing a blue garment of any kind.)*

"EDIE"

We all went to private schools. Kate and I went to the same school that my mother, my aunts, and my grandmother, for God's sake, went to. There never was any doubt that we Barnett girls would go. Of course, I did start attending when I was in the first grade. I mean, how rebellious can one be at that age about things like that?

CHIP

Hi, little one. How was school today?

YOUNG EDIE

Crummy.

CHIP

Oh, I see.

YOUNG EDIE

You don't see anything. You're just smug because you're already out for spring break.

CHIP

You're out now, aren't you?

YOUNG EDIE

Big deal.

KATE

Did you say hello to Miss Babcock for me?

YOUNG EDIE

Yeah, and I got yelled at, too.

KATE

From Miss Babcock?

*(*Young Edie *nods.)*

Why?

YOUNG EDIE

My shirt tail was out. Why else? Dumb old school. Why can't we be like normal people?

(Lights up on the apartment. Edie *is on the phone.)*

EDIE

Janet? I . . . It's Edie. My God, it hasn't been that long, has it, since my birthday party? . . . Well . . . I . . . was wondering . . .
. . . Oh, right, Florida . . .

(Lights fade down on the apartment. The scene continues downstairs.)

KATE

Could Edie be in one of her moods?

"EDIE"

It was bad enough to be deemed moody, but everyone insisted on telling me that I was whether I was or not.

YOUNG EDIE

(Out of the blue)

I'm not going with you to Aspen.

CHIP

You know, I think you're impossible just to be impossible. We all know you love to ski more than almost anything else, so don't try and fool us.

KATE

Let it be, Chip.

CHIP

No, I'm really tired of her crap. Life is so God-damned dramatic for her. You'd think she was like that comic book character, Richie Rich, poor little rich girl. Do something about your misery, don't just wallow in it. You don't see me just sitting around moping, do you? I'm going to do something with my life.

(Lights fade up on the apartment. Edie *is still on the phone.)*

EDIE

You got that job . . . Oh, really? How nice. That sounds great . . . I . . . Chip? Oh, well, it's official now. He's joined Daddy's firm . . . Who knows if it's what he wants? I mean, what else is he going to do?

"EDIE"

Chip had every intention of becoming an archaeologist. He was very excited by the romance and mystery of Leake's work.

EDIE

. . . Yeah, I gotta go, too . . . Right, soon, I promise . . .

(Lights fade out completely on the apartment.)

KATE

Between the two of you, I don't see how anybody can get any work done. If you ask me, you both deserve each other.

YOUNG EDIE

That just shows you how much you know.

KATE

Are you packed yet?

YOUNG EDIE

I told you. I'm not going.

*(*Chip *groans loudly.)*

KATE

(Shouts offstage)

Mother, I think you need to talk to Edie.

MARIAN

(Offstage)

Now what is it.

CHIP

It's nothing new, believe me.

(He exits upstairs.)

KATE

I don't know, but she claims she doesn't want to go to Aspen with us.

MARIAN

(Enters from kitchen.)

Is that true, Edith?

(Both "Edie" *and* Young Edie *wince.)*

YOUNG EDIE

Is what true?

MARIAN

That you don't want to go with us?

YOUNG EDIE

Maybe.

MARIAN

(Sighs)

Why not?

YOUNG EDIE

(Blurts it out)

Because . . . because if I don't go on vacation, then I won't know when it ends, and if I don't know when it ends, then I won't have to go back to school. That's why.

MARIAN

Oh, I see, we're back to that again, are we?

YOUNG EDIE

Yes, we are. Can't I go somewhere else?

MARIAN

You wouldn't go away to boarding school.

YOUNG EDIE

I know, but maybe I've changed my mind.

MARIAN

You agreed to stick it out for the rest of the year without a fuss.

YOUNG EDIE

But, Mom, it gets worse every day. Why do I have to stay there? I think you like torturing me.

MARIAN

We do. It's true, you know. Your father and I get a particular pleasure knowing that you are writhing and sweating it out at one of the best preparatory schools in the country.

YOUNG EDIE

Very funny, Mom. You should be on TV.

MARIAN

Edie, just trust us for once. Believe me when I say we think it is very good for you. You'll thank us for it someday.

KATE

She's right, you know.

"EDIE"

(Realizing it for the first time)

Yes, she was.

YOUNG EDIE

That doesn't mean anything to me right now.

MARIAN

Maybe not.

KATE

Jesus, Edie, what is your problem? I thought Chatham was great. Why, if it hadn't been for Miss Babcock and her Women in Lit class . . .

YOUNG EDIE

You can have your precious Miss Babcock. She's four years older now and eighty times more senile. It's not healthy for a young girl to be exposed to people like her.

MARIAN

Edith, are you making a serious accusation?

MARIAN

No, she's just mad at the entire world today. Especially Miss Babcock.

(Lights fade up on the apartment. Edie *and* Jessie *are sitting on the couch, drinking beer.* "Edie" *will begin to pay particular attention to* Edie's *constant drinking.)*

EDIE

God, I hated that woman. We had to write what we thought our ideal utopia would be. I guess we were reading Jonathan Swift or Thomas More. I never could keep any of that stuff straight. Well, I wrote mine and then we had to read them aloud, or at least tell about them. She told me in front of the whole class that it was the stupidest utopia she ever heard. Well, it was my fucking utopia. How dare she criticize what I wanted?

(Lights fade out on the apartment.)

MARIAN

Well, I hope you all are ready to go when your father gets home. We want to be able to hit those slopes bright and early tomorrow.

YOUNG EDIE

I'm still not going.

MARIAN

Of course you are. You will go and you will have a good time. We'll discuss this other matter some other time, o.k.?

YOUNG EDIE

This isn't the last time you'll hear from me.

MARIAN

I'm sure of that. Come on, everybody, snap to.

*(*Kate *and* Marian *begin to exit.)*

Edith, that means you, too.

YOUNG EDIE

I hate skiing.

MARIAN

Nonsense.

(Lights fade out on living room as Young Edie *resignedly climbs stairs. Spotlight finds* "Edie."*)*

"EDIE"

Needless to say, life did indeed push onward. We went to Aspen, as we always did; I had a wonderful time, as I always did. I even stopped being mad at Miss Babcock. There came a truce. I began to do what was expected, I think, but . . .

(Lights fade up on the apartment. Jessie *and* Edie *are in the living room.* Edie *is lying down on the couch.)*

JESSIE

Come on, Edie, quit moping around. You remind me of that comic book character, Sad Sack.

EDIE

I am not moping.

(Clearly, she is.)

JESSIE

All right, pouting then.

EDIE

No.

JESSIE

Well, I am not a psychiatrist, so either tell me about the problem or get over it.

EDIE

I will not "get over it" until I'm good and ready.

"EDIE"

A stubborn phase, I see.

JESSIE

Ah, I get it. We're in one of those moods, are we?

"EDIE"

Moody again. When in doubt, I was always moody again.

EDIE

No.

JESSIE

Edie, for crying out loud, cut it out.

EDIE

No.

(Jessie throws her a look. She sighs, then rolls over onto her back.)

I hate my life.

JESSIE

Now, we're getting somewhere. What are you talking about? You have a great life.

EDIE

Had.

"EDIE"

Had?

EDIE

Had. My life is over.

JESSIE

Well, if that don't beat all.

EDIE

Doesn't.

JESSIE

Does too.

EDIE

No, dope. "Doesn't beat all," not "don't beat all."

JESSIE

O.k., I'm going to walk right into this with both eyes open. Tell me, why is your life over?

EDIE

All the simple things are done.

(Lights fade up on the living room. Young Edie *enters from the front door, slams it.)*

YOUNG EDIE

Mother, hey, Mom.

MARIAN

(Enters from the kitchen, with mail in her hand. She proceeds to the desk to take care of the correspondence while the scene continues.)

Yes, dear, what is it?

YOUNG EDIE

Jessie's asked me to his senior prom. Isn't that great?

JESSIE

That's the stupidest thing I've ever heard.

MARIAN

I suppose.

EDIE

No, I mean it. I've done all the things I've ever wanted to do. I don't know where to go from here.

JESSIE

Jesus H. Christ, Edie. You're only twenty-three. You can do whatever you want to do. What about your photography?

EDIE

I hate that job. I'm serious, Jess. How do I know what I want to do until I do whatever it is that I think I want to do to find out if I really wanted to do it in the first place?

*(*Jessie *shakes his head at her as the lights fade out on the apartment. The scene continues downstairs.)*

YOUNG EDIE

This means I'll need a new dress, you know.

MARIAN

We'll have to talk to your father about that.

"EDIE"

Piece of cake. That meant I would get it.

MARIAN

I'm not sure, however, he will even approve of you going to Jessie's prom.

YOUNG EDIE

Why not?

"EDIE"

I always thought Jessie was safe. At least, his family belonged to the right clubs.

MARIAN

I don't know, dear. He's very protective of you sometimes.

YOUNG EDIE

He never was like this with Kate.

MARIAN

He didn't have to be. She was a little more sensible.

YOUNG EDIE

What you really mean is that she didn't have any dates.

"EDIE"

In my mind, sensible meant boring and unpopular and I was determined never to let that be said about me.

MARIAN

Edith.

YOUNG EDIE

I'm sorry, but it's true.

MARIAN

True or not, it was uncalled for.

Young Edie

Yes, ma'am.

Marian

We'll continue this other discussion when your father gets home.

(Lights fade out on the living room. Lights fade up on the apartment.)

Jessie

You make no sense sometimes.

"Edie"

I thought I always made sense.

Edie

I'm scared, Jess. I'm really scared.

Jessie

Of what?

Edie

Just hold me, o.k.?

*(*Jessie *crosses to her and hugs her. Lights fade out on apartment as they fade up on living room.* Charles, Marian, Chip, Kate, *and* Young Edie *are in the living room. It is after dinner.)*

Charles

Well, Chipper, looks like you are rounding third and heading for home, eh?

Chip

Sir?

Charles

I meant it's your last semester in college.

Chip

Ah, yes, sir, it is.

Charles

Have we thought any more about what we are going to do after we graduate?

"EDIE"

Note the Victorian phrasing. Significant.

CHIP

Actually, we, er, I mean, I have.

YOUNG EDIE

He wants to take off and find himself, Daddy.

CHIP

Shut up, you little brat.

YOUNG EDIE

Well, I can't help listening to this stupid conversation.

MARIAN

This conversation is not meant for you, Edith.

"EDIE"

I never could understand why we always talked about everything in front of everyone, yet expected those not directly involved not to listen. I mean we discussed everything except . . .

CHARLES

What will you do for money?

"EDIE"

Bingo.

MARIAN

Don't be crass, dear.

CHARLES

Well, if he is serious about this, he will have to think about putting bread in his mouth.

YOUNG EDIE

Ha. Look at him, he could do without . . .

CHARLES

Edith.

YOUNG EDIE AND "EDIE"

Ooops.

CHIP

I'm really not sure what I want to do. It was just a thought.

MARIAN

Well, I think it's a great idea.

CHARLES

What is?

MARIAN

If Chip wants to go off, travel a bit, do whatever he fancies.

CHARLES

Well, I fancy that I'm not going to support this kind of irresponsible . . .

"EDIE"

You know, even as much as I love my father, I always thought that at least he would understand.

CHIP

I have not asked anybody for any money. Geez.

KATE

My advice, dear brother, is to stay in school. Go get a master's. He'll probably support that.

"EDIE"

Always practical, that one.

CHARLES

Well, then, what are you asking for?

CHIP

Nothing. Sir, I don't believe since this conversation began, I have asked for anything.

MARIAN

He's right, you know.

YOUNG EDIE

What's the big deal? When he gets hungry enough, he'll come crawling back. Isn't that what you want?

MARIAN AND KATE

Edith.

CHARLES

Certainly not.

"EDIE"

The "baby" speaks the truth.

CHIP

Oh, forget it, just forget it

(Chip exits.)

MARIAN

Now, Chip, don't be that way.

(She follows him.)

CHARLES

Kate, is that what he really wants to do?

KATE

I don't think he really knows yet what he wants to do.

CHARLES

Well, what does one do with an archaeology degree anyway?

(Lights fade out on the living room and fade up on the apartment. Jessie *is holding* Edie.*)*

EDIE

. . . and after you've done what it is you think you want to do and find out that it really wasn't what you wanted to do, then what do you do? What do you want from there?

JESSIE

Keep plugging away, I guess. Ideas will come to you.

EDIE

That's not what I mean. There are plenty of things that I know that I want to do. I never run out of those kinds of ideas. But what I mean is the big want, the one for the rest of your life. What do you do when that one is gone?

JESSIE

Edie, you don't just wake up one day, like the day you graduate and say, "O.k., I'm going to be an airline stewardess for the rest of my life." It just doesn't work like that. You'll change, you'll change your mind. Lord knows, you'll change your mind, and the world will change. Nobody said it had to be permanent. Just go along with something until it doesn't feel right anymore.

EDIE

What about being a doctor? Isn't that for life?

JESSIE

For me it is.

EDIE

But "why," Jess?

JESSIE

I don't know. It's always been that way. I guess I've always known what I wanted.

EDIE

My point exactly. I don't have "being a doctor" on my horizon.

JESSIE

Not everybody does. Not everybody can. It's a totally different thing from what you're talking about.

EDIE

I don't think so and I want to have that. I want to know the "why."

(Lights fade slowly on apartment. Light hits Edie.*)*

"EDIE"

I always hated playing gin rummy. There were too many options, too many potential possible combinations that I went crazy trying to decide which ones to wait for and which ones to discard. Now, gin, gin was more my style. It was over when it was over. You made a decision and you had to stick with it.

(Lights fade up on the living room. Young Edie *and* Janet *are making signs. They are in school uniforms.)*

YOUNG EDIE

You know, I don't know what I would have done if you hadn't agreed to be my campaign manager.

JANET

I didn't realize that there was any choice in the matter.

YOUNG EDIE

Janet Townsend. You are, after all, my best friend in the whole world. What do you mean by "choice in the matter"? Didn't you want to do it?

JANET

Well, sure, I guess so.

YOUNG EDIE

Thanks a lot. I wouldn't have run if I couldn't have had you.

JANET

You mean it, Edie?

YOUNG EDIE

Honor bright, idiot.

"EDIE"

An "honor bright" is stronger than a promise. One can always break a promise, but if one gives an honor bright, well . . . one better mean it.

YOUNG EDIE

We're a pair — Tweedledee and Tweedledum. How could I go into the field of battle without my best bud?

JANET

I never thought of it that way.

YOUNG EDIE

Yeah, well, you should have.

JANET

How about "What We Need Is Our Ede"?

YOUNG EDIE

You know, you may be a great campaign manager, but slogans you're a little weak on.

JANET

Let's see you do better.

YOUNG EDIE

Uhm . . . "Bar None, BarNett Is the One."

*(*Janet *rolls her eyes.)*

YOUNG EDIE

Pretty bad, huh?

*(*Janet *nods. Lights fade down, but not out, on them as they continue to make signs, showing them to each other. Spot hits* "Edie."*)*

"EDIE"

I wonder what great office I'm running for. I tried for everything — student council, president of the class. No, actually, Janet ran for that one. We thought it would be great if the two of us had the highest offices in school. We knew we could run the school better than anybody else.

("Edie" *has been watching* Young Edie *and* Janet *as they have been holding up the signs.)*

Ah, now I remember this one. Blue team captain. You see, half the school was divided into blue, and the other half into white. I never did figure out the rationale for that one.

(Lights begin a slow fade out downstairs as we hear Edie *in the apartment humming a camp tune.* Jessie *is still there with her.)*

EDIE

Isn't it crazy how I remember those songs? Camp seems so long ago.

JESSIE

I think that was a very happy time for you.

EDIE

No, it wasn't. I was miserable.

"EDIE"

Now somebody get their stories straight. Was I or wasn't I . . . ?

JESSIE

Make up your mind.

"EDIE"

I thought I had.

EDIE

Quit picking on me. I never pick on you the way you always do me.

JESSIE

Well, there are certain people in this world who just beg to be picked on and you're one of them.

EDIE

How come you have no faults, or problems, even? You know, in the million or so years that we have been seeing each other, I don't believe you've ever had a problem.

JESSIE

Ever?

EDIE

Well, I mean, at least not a major problem. Have you?

JESSIE

(Thinks a minute)

Nope, I guess not.

EDIE

Why in the hell not?

JESSIE

How should I know? It's not a crime, you know, not having problems. I guess I seem to handle things differently from you. Everything always seems to fall into place for me.

EDIE

Oh, now I can't handle my life. Is that what you're saying?

JESSIE

Oh, Jesus. Settle down, timba. It's just that . . . Oh, never mind.

EDIE

It is difficult for me, you know.

JESSIE

(Softly and very understanding)

Yes, I know.

"EDIE"

Why?

(Lights fade out on the apartment. We begin to hear the piano as lights fade up on the living room. It is Kate *playing.* Young Edie *bursts into the room from the front door, wearing a gym tunic and carrying a tennis racket.)*

YOUNG EDIE

(She sees Kate.*)*

Katie, Katie, guess what?

KATE

(Never one to panic, she continues playing without missing a beat.)

What, Edie?

YOUNG EDIE

I won, I won.

(She is skipping around the room.)

KATE

Hold still at least. It's hard enough to look at you when I'm trying to practice. Won what, sweetie?

YOUNG EDIE

Only the most important thing in the world to me.

"EDIE"

It is at times like these that you wish, upon reflecting, that you weren't so ingratiatingly adolescent.

KATE

Which is . . . ?

YOUNG EDIE

The tennis tournament, stupie. God, if you'd only been paying attention for the last two weeks, you'd have known what I'm talking about.

KATE

This may come as quite a shock to you, but not everyone in this house hangs on your every word to make or break their day.

YOUNG EDIE

You don't understand anything, do you?

KATE

Au contraire, I believe that I understand a great deal.

YOUNG EDIE

Where's Mom?

KATE

She had some shopping to do.

YOUNG EDIE

Damn it, of all the times to be gone . . .

KATE

Edith.

*(*Kate *finally stops playing.)*

YOUNG EDIE

(Exasperated, she exhales quickly, causing her lips to flap together, making a kind of horse sound.)

Not you, too. Don't start in on me like that.

KATE

Sorry. What's so important?

YOUNG EDIE

Well, there's this party tonight for all the winners of the spring sports meet and I thought since I won the tennis, I should go . . .

KATE

I don't know that that's such a hot idea.

YOUNG EDIE

Why not? I ought to go. Besides, it'll look bad if the captain of the blue team doesn't even show up for her own party.

KATE

Oh, you're giving it now, are you?

YOUNG EDIE

Not really, but it's over at Janet's house, so it's practically the same thing.

KATE

Oh, I see. Well, I still don't think Mom will let you go.

YOUNG EDIE

Again I ask, why not?

KATE

Have you forgotten that it is Grandmother's birthday?

YOUNG EDIE

So?

KATE

Her eightieth birthday? And we, as in "the entire family," are throwing her a party at the club, tonight, remember?

YOUNG EDIE

Oh, crime, I can't believe this is happening to me. Do I really have to go? I mean, everyone else will . . .

KATE

(Shoots her a look)

Everyone will be there. Everyone.

YOUNG EDIE

I know. Do you think that you could call her . . .

KATE

No.

YOUNG EDIE

I didn't think so. How about I'm sick? You know, sudden flu . . .

KATE

No, Edie.

YOUNG EDIE

How can you be so cruel? To your own sister?

KATE

Now, Edie, be fair. You have to go. You know you have to go.

YOUNG EDIE

(Heavy sigh)

I know, I know.

KATE

You'll have other parties. You'll probably win other awards. But tonight is rather special for Grandmother, too.

YOUNG EDIE

Yeah, I suppose.

*(*Kate *resumes playing.)*

"EDIE"

Points scored on me were hard won and begrudgingly given.

YOUNG EDIE

What are you playing?

KATE

Some Brahms.

YOUNG EDIE

Hard?

KATE

No, want to try?

YOUNG EDIE

No, I can't do that stuff anymore.

KATE

(She shuffles through some music scores.)

I've got a better idea. Let's play one of those four hard numbers we used to play.

*(*Young Edie *hesitates.)*

Come on, it'll be fun.

YOUNG EDIE

O.k., but only if I get to play the bottom hand.

KATE

(Smiles)

Of course.

(They begin to play. Lights fade on the living room and fade up on the apartment. Edie *is talking on the phone.)*

EDIE

Hey, Janet? I can't go to MIT tonight like we planned . . . I know, but you'll be fine. There's lots of people you know going . . . Because my stupid sister . . .

"EDIE"

(Overlapping)

Stupid?

EDIE

. . . is in town this weekend. She showed up unexpectedly. I sort of have to entertain her, I guess . . . We're going to the symphony, so you're on your own. Don't do anything I wouldn't do . . . What do you mean you're not going? It's the "Spring Fling," for God's sake.

Of course, you're going. You will go and you will have a good time . . . Because I want to hear all about it. Call me later. I want all the gory details.

(Lights fade out on the apartment. The spot finds "Edie."*)*

"EDIE"

I may have been a whiz on the old athletic fields but the old brain was no match. I've been called clever, mischievous, moody, even sly, but intellectual I definitely was not. Regardless of SAT scores, however, the point in my family was not that you were going to college, but, rather, which college.

(Lights fade up on the living room. Charles, Marian, Kate, *and* Young Edie *are relaxing after dinner.)*

YOUNG EDIE

(Out of the blue)

I've decided that I want to go to Rollins.

MARIAN AND CHARLES

What?

YOUNG EDIE

Rollins, you know, that college in Florida.

CHARLES

You mean that water ski school?

MARIAN

Charles. Edie, whatever gave you such an idea?

YOUNG EDIE

Well, Miss Haynes said that I have to be practical about picking colleges, which means she thinks I'm going to have trouble getting into a good school.

CHARLES

That is ridiculous. I've never heard of such a thing.

YOUNG EDIE

Just because you give Brown and Wheaton a ton of money every year does not necessarily mean that your retarded offspring automatically will be accepted with open arms.

CHARLES

Edie, you are not retarded. I won't have you talk that way.

YOUNG EDIE

Oh, yeah, have you looked at my board scores recently?

("Edie" rolls her eyes upward.)

CHARLES

Well, maybe slightly slow.

YOUNG EDIE

Daddy.

MARIAN

Charles.

CHARLES

Just teasing, but I can tell you one thing — and that is that Rollins is definitely out of the question.

YOUNG EDIE

Well, dumb old Miss Haynes said she won't even let me apply in the east.

CHARLES

What? That is utter nonsense.

YOUNG EDIE

She didn't say I couldn't apply; she just said she wouldn't help. Big diff.

MARIAN

Why not, dear?

YOUNG EDIE

I don't know. Something about percentages and making sure everyone gets accepted somewhere. They don't care where you go, as long as you at least get in somewhere.

KATE

That's not entirely true, Edie.

*(*Young Edie *shrugs.)*

Have you ever thought that maybe Miss Haynes really has your best interests at heart? I mean, you didn't exactly shine academically, and maybe she doesn't think you really care to go to a tough school.

YOUNG EDIE

Well, God, thanks a lot. Whose side are you on, anyway?

KATE

You brought it up.

MARIAN

Girls, please. Now, Edie, just what exactly did Miss Haynes say about your chances of getting into Wheaton?

CHARLES

To hell with that, try for the top. What did she say about Brown?

"EDIE"

Sometimes I felt like I was in a bridge game and couldn't get back to the board.

YOUNG EDIE

To hell with it.

MARIAN

Edith.

YOUNG EDIE

Ugh. I'm taking a year off.

CHARLES

You can't.

YOUNG EDIE

Why not? Chip is.

CHARLES

I won't let you. That's why not.

YOUNG EDIE

Now I'm getting real confused.

(She closes her eyes and snaps her fingers.)

(Lights fade out on the living room. The spot finds "Edie.")

"EDIE"

Didn't you think that at age eighteen you knew everything? I know I did. This was at a time in my life when I couldn't believe that they didn't know, that they had forgotten and it was making my life more difficult trying to constantly explain what I thought was perfectly logical. I wished sometimes that I could snap my fingers and they would all disappear. Then I could do what I wanted to do. And when I was lonely or needed them, I could just snap my fingers again and the ones I wanted would appear, until I couldn't stand them anymore. That, by the way, was my "stupid" utopia.

(As "Edie" continues to speak, the lights fade up on the living room. The front door opens and Young Edie and Jessie enter. They are very playful with one another. Young Edie is trying to tickle Jessie and dodges him as he tries to catch her. He finally does catch her, they wrestle a bit and then he pins her down.)

JESSIE

Well, what are you going to do?

YOUNG EDIE

I don't think there is much I can do at this point, is there? Do I have to say "uncle"?

JESSIE

No, I meant about college.

(He lets her go.)

YOUNG EDIE

Oh, that. I don't know. Janet's going to Wellesley.

JESSIE

Well . . . ?

YOUNG EDIE

All girls.

JESSIE

Right.

YOUNG EDIE

Miss Haynes suggested Simmons.

JESSIE

I thought that was all girls, too.

YOUNG EDIE

I know, but since you'll be at Harvard, I thought I would like to be in Boston, and I think I could probably get in.

JESSIE

There are other schools in Boston, you know.

*(*Young Edie *shrugs.)*

Well, do what you want.

"EDIE"

Good boy, he knew I would anyway.

YOUNG EDIE

Besides, I can always transfer.

"EDIE"

Hallelujah, praise the Lord, the decision has been made. Off to Simmons we go.

(Lights fade out on the living room while the spot remains on "Edie."*)*

I hear you. Simmons, you say. I know, I know, but it gets back to two things: gin and Jessie.

("Edie"*'s spot goes to black as the lights fade up*

on the apartment. Edie *is on the phone. It rings downstairs as the lights fade up on the living room. We see* Charles *and* Marian *sitting.* Charles *answers the phone.)*

CHARLES

Hello.

EDIE

Daddy? It's me.

CHARLES

Hello, baby, how are you?

MARIAN

Edith?

(Charles *nods yes.)*

EDIE

I'm fine, sir.

CHARLES

How much?

EDIE

How did you know?

CHARLES

"Sir" — dead giveaway.

MARIAN

How much?

(Charles *shakes his head.)*

EDIE

I don't know where it all goes, Daddy.

CHARLES

Maybe you ought to keep a record for a month and find out.

EDIE

Would it make a difference?

CHARLES

I doubt it. You give to any stray on the street. Perhaps a little discretion with your causes would help.

EDIE

I can't help it. I see a hand and I have to give.

CHARLES

You don't have to.

EDIE

Yes, yes, I do.

CHARLES

But then, you have nothing for yourself.

EDIE

I get by.

CHARLES

I hardly call phoning home every month or so . . .

EDIE

Please, don't start in on this again. Not tonight.

MARIAN

How's her job?

CHARLES

How's your job?

EDIE

(Quick sigh)

I quit.

CHARLES

Edie . . .

EDIE

Well, actually, they let me go.

*(*Charles *looks at* Marian *and whispers, "She lost her job."* Marian *shakes her head.)*

But, I'm trying to find another one. I am. You don't know how hard it is. I have no marketable skills. People don't care who you are and what you are — just can you program a computer. And I'd like it once, just once, that my name carried some weight around here. Who the hell are we, anyway? And if we're supposed to be somebody, why isn't it helping me?

CHARLES

Now, Edie . . .

EDIE

I mean, I'm not asking for much. If I have to have an inane job where I am a vegetable and push paper, then pay me a good wage for there is a mind wasting here, or so I'm told; or if I get a job that uses my supposed skills, then fine — I'll work for practically nothing. But, for some reason, I can't find either. And I want to know why. Why can't I have that? You didn't exactly have to worry and look where you are.

CHARLES

Whoa, hold it right there, young lady. First of all, that's not entirely true. Your mother and I have had our rough times, believe me.

EDIE

Oh, yeah, for about ten minutes.

CHARLES

Look, I don't appreciate your abuse. I sympathize with you, but don't forget, it was you who called me, not the reverse and I think you had better calm down right now before you continue . . .

EDIE

Are you threatening me?

CHARLES

Of course not.

(Clearly he is, but he calms down as quickly as he angered.)

I think we're both getting a little excited here. Perhaps you'd like to talk to your mother.

*(*Charles *waves* Marian *over to the phone.)*

EDIE

(Under her breath)

Great.

MARIAN

(To Charles*)*

What's wrong?

CHARLES

I'm not quite sure.

(He goes to make himself another drink.)

MARIAN

Edith, how are you, dear?

EDIE

You couldn't tell?

MARIAN

Well, my version was rather one-sided. Are you all right now?

"EDIE"

They always expected these outbursts to go away as fast as they came.

EDIE

Yes, Mother, I'm fine. I need some money.

MARIAN

Oh, is that all?

*(*Charles *winces.)*

EDIE

Is that all? That may be easy for you to say, but there is a lot behind all this grovelling . . .

MARIAN

No need for hysterics. How much, dear?

EDIE

I don't know. Maybe a couple of hundred. That should hold me for awhile.

MARIAN

I'll send you a check for five hundred. Will that be all right?

EDIE

Yes, Mother, thank you. That will be fine. I . . . I . . . appreciate it.

MARIAN

I trust you will put it to constructive use.

EDIE

As always.

MARIAN

That's what I'm afraid of.

*(*Edie *inhales a quick breath and slowly lets it out, almost in a sigh.)*

Call us again on a more cheerful note, o.k.? We miss you.

EDIE

Yes, Mother. Thanks again. Say goodbye to Daddy for me. I've got to go.

MARIAN

Goodnight.

*(*Edie *and* Marian *hang up. Lights fade out on the living room.* Edie *looks at the phone for a minute, shakes her head and crosses to the kitchen for a drink.* "Edie" *observes* Edie. *Lights on the apartment and the spot fades to black. Lights fade up on the living room.* Young Edie *and* Janet *enter from the kitchen with beers and a bag of potato chips.)*

YOUNG EDIE

I told them no way, no way was I going to do it.

JANET

And they said o.k.?

YOUNG EDIE

Of course.

JANET

I wish it were that easy for me.

YOUNG EDIE

Look, Janet, face it. Yours aren't as well trained as mine.

JANET

I guess not.

YOUNG EDIE

It must be tough being the oldest. I mean, mine are too tired to deal with me.

JANET

Boy, are you lucky. So, have you seen what I'm going to wear?

YOUNG EDIE

Let me guess. Is it white?

JANET

Very funny. How many choices does one have?

YOUNG EDIE

I am so glad that it's you and not me. Did you have to go to that fashion show?

JANET

No, thank God.

YOUNG EDIE

Yeah, well, my mom dragged me.

JANET

Really? Why?

YOUNG EDIE

I think she thought I would get "inspired" and change my mind. Ugh. I mean, it was like such a big deal. Everyone you've known for ages and thought were fairly reasonable and rational were giggling and gushing away like . . . well, I don't know what like.

JANET

Sounded pretty awful.

YOUNG EDIE

I hadn't seen that much pink and green in one place since the new Papagallos store opened up last year.

JANET

Unbelievable.

YOUNG EDIE

Really. Tell me about it.

*(*Young Edie *is just about to put her feet up on the coffee table.)*

SARAH

(Offstage)

Edie, you get your feet off the furniture and don't go leaving any rings on the table.

(Both Young Edie *and* Janet *remove their beers from the coffee table. As* Sarah *continues,* Young Edie *and* Janet *quietly sneak upstairs.)*

Your mother and father are having a fancy party tonight and you know how your mother gets.

*(*Sarah *enters from the kitchen in formal maid's uniform.)*

Hmm. About time that child listened to me.

(She picks up the bag of potato chips, eats one, and exits to the kitchen, muttering to herself.)

(Lights on the living room fade to black. Lights on the apartment fade up to reveal Edie *alone, drinking. Lights quickly fade up on the living room.*

Charles and Chip are in tails. Marian and Kate are in long formal gowns. Sarah is serving hors d'oeuvres from a silver tray.)

CHARLES

So, where's the little deb?

"EDIE"

O.k., go ahead, laugh, but, you see, the Barnetts' debut — that was a fact, not an option.

KATE

I don't think I'd say that very loudly if I were you, Dad.

CHARLES

Why not?

CHIP

The little deb's not in a very good mood.

CHARLES

Ah, another one of her moods.

"EDIE"

"Wolf."

KATE

Well, I think what set it off was going to the hair dresser this morning.

CHARLES

(Confused)

Yes, I can see how that would put her in a bad mood.

KATE

Well, she really looked nice when she first came home, didn't she, Chip?

CHIP

How would I know anything about that kind of thing?

KATE

Well, she did. It was curled just right and she seemed pretty pleased with herself, didn't she, Chip?

CHIP

She always seems pretty pleased with herself, if you ask me.

CHARLES

Nobody's asked you.

CHIP

Sorry, sir.

CHARLES

So what's the big trauma. So far, everything sounds grand.

SARAH

The bath.

CHARLES

What?

SARAH

The bath she took when she got home.

CHARLES

(Still not catching on)

Huh?

KATE

You see, when she took that long, hot, steamy bath . . .

CHIP

All her hair fell out.

CHARLES

All her hair . . . ?

KATE

(Hits Chip*)*

Not literally. There isn't much curl to it now and it's kind of . . . well, let's just say that there isn't much life to it.

CHIP

To be perfectly honest, she looks downright awful.

CHARLES

I'm sure that your mother can salvage something. Sarah, do you think you could go upstairs and see what is taking them so long.

SARAH

Certainly, sir.

(She exits upstairs.)

"EDIE"

I figured everyone was secretly getting a big kick out of this little scene. I did look like a drowned rat — there was no getting around that fact. My brother particularly thought it was hysterical, but he wasn't too happy later after I punched him in the stomach for drinking too much and making a fool out of himself. It was, after all, still my party. I had some pride.

CHARLES

(Shouting upstairs)

Marian, what the devil is taking so long? We're going to be late for the pre-party pictures.

MARIAN

(Offstage)

We'll be along soon.

(Focus shifts to the apartment. Edie *is on the phone.)*

EDIE

Hello, Sarah? . . . It's me. Listen, are they home? . . . Was that tonight? . . . No, I guess I forgot . . . Nothing special . . . Yes, that would be fine. Bye.

(She hangs up, snaps her fingers and looks around. She then crosses to the kitchen, refills her drink, and crosses back to the couch.)

(Meanwhile, the doorbell downstairs has rung. Chip *answers it. It is* Jessie, *dressed in tails. He is*

carrying a magnum bottle of champagne and a Polaroid camera.)

JESSIE

(He holds up the bottle.)

I thought we'd start the evening off right. That is, if you don't object, sir.

CHARLES

Hell, of course not. Best idea we've had around here all day.

JESSIE

Where's the little deb?

CHARLES

Bad question, son. Seems her hair has fallen and she has progressed steadily downhill ever since. Sarah?

(He begins to look for some champagne glasses.)

SARAH

(She pokes her head downstairs.)

Yes, sir?

CHARLES

How's it coming up there?

SARAH

She says she's going to throw up. Neither Mrs. B nor I seem to be able to do anything with her.

JESSIE

May I try? We've been through this sort of thing before.

CHARLES

Be my guest. Sarah, where in blazes do we keep the champagne glasses?

SARAH

Coming, sir.

(She comes downstairs and finds the glasses. Jessie *has exited upstairs.)*

CHIP

We never had this much trouble with your debut, did we, Kate?

KATE

Squelch it, Chip.

(Marian *enters from upstairs.)*

CHARLES

What's going on up there? Doesn't she know that we have to be there at six-thirty and it's almost a quarter past now?

MARIAN

You want to tell her?

(All of a sudden, we hear the sound of a door being flung open, a shout, and the sound of two people rushing down the stairs. Jessie *first, with the camera in his hand. The little deb is in hot pursuit.)*

YOUNG EDIE

(Offstage)

You God-damn son of a bitch. You come back here.

(Jessie *enters the living room and immediately hides behind* Charles.*)*

JESSIE

Sir, I value my life. Amnesty, please.

CHARLES

What did you do?

JESSIE

I got her out of the bathroom.

(Young Edie *enters in a white debutante gown. Her hair is, indeed, a mess. It looks like they tried to rewet it and hadn't finished the job. In spite of that, however, she does look quite elegant.)*

YOUNG EDIE

Daddy, don't protect that creep. Hand him over.

*(*Young Edie *starts to dodge around her father to get to* Jessie, *but* Charles *is very adept at fending her off.)*

Give me that picture.

CHARLES

Calm down, Edie.

YOUNG EDIE

Calm down? He only took a picture of me hanging over a toilet bowl with hair of death and a crummy white dress on. Talk about blackmail potential and you tell me to calm down?

CHARLES

Surely, Jessie wouldn't do such a thing.

YOUNG EDIE

Ha, your problem is that you like him. Believe me, he's not all goodness and light.

*(*Young Edie *realizes that she is getting nowhere. She stops trying to get to* Jessie.*)*

All right. I'll make a deal with both of you. I'll calm down, if you just give me the picture.

*(*Charles *and* Jessie *go into a huddle.)*

CHARLES

Sounds fair to me. What do you say, Jessie?

*(*Jessie *looks skeptical. He waves the picture over her head. She tries to grab it, but he puts it out of her reach.)*

JESSIE

You promise to behave for the rest of the night? No funny business?

YOUNG EDIE

I promise.

(She grabs for the picture, but he still holds it. He looks at her as if there is more for her to say.)

YOUNG EDIE

(Sighs)

Honor bright.

*(*Jessie *hands her the picture. She grabs it, yells "ahha," and makes a beeline for the stairs.)*

JESSIE

Honor bright, pumpkin.

(His line stops her dead in her tracks. She slowly turns back to them and snaps her fingers. Charles *is unduly impressed.)*

"EDIE"

Utopia time.

*(*Young Edie *heads back into the living room.)*

MARIAN

(To Jessie*)*

I'm not even going to begin to try to know how you did that.

CHARLES

I don't think you look that bad, darling.

YOUNG EDIE

Hummpf.

CHARLES

Well, time for one round, don't you think?

*(*Sarah *begins distributing champagne. Everyone, including* "Edie," *takes one.* Edie *has refilled her drink again and crosses to the center of her apartment.* Young Edie *reaches for a glass.)*

CHARLES

Not for you, young lady. We can't have you tripping down those stairs.

YOUNG EDIE

I suppose champagne helps you keep your balance.

MARIAN

Let her have one. After all, you did let Katherine drink that night.

CHARLES

I suppose I did. Let's make a toast. Everyone got glasses? You, too, Sarah. Grab a glass.

SARAH

Oh, Mr. Barnett.

(To Young Edie*)*

Child, I swear you look prettier than ever.

YOUNG EDIE

You never were a very good liar, Sarah, but thanks, anyway.

MARIAN

Edith.

(All three Edies wince.)

CHARLES

A toast. To the last little deb.

(With that, everyone, including "Edie" *and* Edie, *raises their glasses.)*

CHARLES, "EDIE," AND EDIE

May she do the Barnetts proud.

*(*Everyone, *except the three Edies, freezes with glasses raised. Lights become specials on the three.* Young Edie *finishes her champagne in one gulp, hikes up her skirt, and exits out the front door.* Edie *finishes her drink, snaps her fingers twice, looks around, and slowly sinks to the floor in a sob.* "Edie" *finishes her champagne, quickly tosses her glass over her shoulder, and, realizing what she has done, freezes with a frontal stare to the audience.)*

(Lights fade to black.)

(End of Act One.*)*

ACT TWO

ACT TWO

SCENE: (Edie's apartment.)

AT RISE: (The entire Barnett family and Jessie are upstairs in Edie's apartment. Charles is attempting to pace with little or no success. "Edie" is in her usual place. It is mid-morning.)

CHARLES

How long is she going to be in there?

JESSIE

Probably five more minutes.

CHARLES

Are you sure?

CHIP

Can you ever be sure about Edie?

CHARLES

Good point. Damn her, has she ever been on time for anything?

MARIAN

Calm down, dear. It's not that late yet.

CHARLES

What does she do in there, anyway?

(Everyone responds to him with a shrug, except Jessie *who begins to answer.)*

JESSIE

Well . . .

CHARLES

(Waves him off)

Never mind. I don't want to know really.

(Meanwhile, downstairs, which is in dark, we hear the sound of the front door opening and closing very softly and slowly. Several beats of silence pass. We hear someone bang into something and a terse, whispered, "Shit." It is Young Edie *trying to sneak back into the house.)*

KATE

This is a lovely apartment, isn't it? It's a shame she's going to have to give it up.

MARIAN

Such a good location.

CHARLES

Such a good price.

JESSIE

Maybe she won't have to. Hasn't she told you yet?

*(*Young Edie *turns on a lamp and crosses to the bar. We see* Sarah *in a chair, fast asleep.)*

MARIAN AND CHARLES

No.

JESSIE

I suppose Edie ought to be the one to tell you, but I think she plans on staying in Boston for awhile.

CHARLES

Oh, really? Why's that?

JESSIE

Two reasons, I think. One, it seems this photography lab here is interested in hiring her . . .

CHARLES

What? A job?

*(*Jessie *nods.)*

Will wonders never cease?

MARIAN

Charles.

CHARLES

And, two . . . ?

JESSIE

Since I'll be at Harvard Med, I've been led to believe that, well . . . you get the idea.

CHARLES

Ah, pretty serious, is it?

MARIAN

Charles, really, what a thing to ask.

CHARLES

Jessie doesn't mind, do you, son?

*(*Young Edie *has made her drink and begins to cross upstairs when she sees* Sarah, *whose presence scares her.* "Edie"*'s attention turns to this scene.)*

YOUNG EDIE	JESSIE
Oh, my God.	No, of course not, sir.

SARAH

(Wakes up)

What? Edie? Lord, you're going to be the death of me yet. What are you doing down here, sneaking around, scaring old ladies to death?

YOUNG EDIE

It was not my main intention to scare you. Besides, why aren't you in your room?

SARAH

I was waiting up for you.

YOUNG EDIE

Oh, really. You don't do a very good mother act, Sarah. I've been home for hours. If I'd've known you were down here, I would have gladly rested your worries and sent you to bed.

CHARLES

(Looks at his watch again)

This is unconscionable. I wish she'd get a watch. That's what I should've gotten her for graduation. What did we give her, Marian?

MARIAN

A camera.

CHARLES

Oh, right. It does everything but fly, I've been told. And about this Boston business. I wish she'd come back home and do those things she's supposed to do. You know . . . well, those, whatever those kinds of things are. You know.

JESSIE

She will if she wants to.

CHARLES

Oh, don't give her an option like that. Her problem is that she doesn't know what she wants.

SARAH

(Watches Young Edie *drink)*

You've been home for awhile, you say?

YOUNG EDIE

Yeah. Hours.

SARAH

How come you're still in your clothes?

YOUNG EDIE

Been reading.

SARAH

I see. And the drink?

YOUNG EDIE

Couldn't sleep.

SARAH

Uhha.

*(*Young Edie *has finished her drink and crosses to mix herself another one. Both* "Edie" *and* Sarah *watch.)*

(Upstairs, the bathroom door bursts open. Enter Edie *in traditional cap and gown.* "Edie"'*s attention shifts to this scene.)*

EDIE

Tada. What do you think? I don't think black's my color.

CHIP

All that time for that?

EDIE

Stuff it, Bro. Hail, hail, the gang's all here. Where's Grandmother?

MARIAN

Five flights of stairs defeated her.

EDIE

Well, she's going to miss all the fun. So, who's ready for champagne?

MARIAN

Charles, what time is it?

CHARLES

Ten-thirty.

MARIAN

Isn't the ceremony at eleven, dear?

EDIE

(She crosses to her kitchen. She gets a bottle of champagne from the refrigerator. She crosses back into the living room with the bottle, some paper cups, and a can of peanuts.)

Yep.

CHARLES

Don't you think we ought to get moving?

EDIE

No sweat. Got tons of time. At least time enough for a quick glass of champagne.

(Holds up the paper cups)

I have class, if nothing else.

SARAH AND MARIAN

Isn't it a little bit early in the morning to be drinking?

*(*Young Edie *and* Edie *shrug.)*

EDIE

Come on, you only live once.

*(*Edie *pours and distributes the champagne.)*

SARAH

Honey, is there something bothering you?

YOUNG EDIE

No.

SARAH

You sure?

YOUNG EDIE

Yeah. Why?

SARAH

No reason.

YOUNG EDIE

(Finishes her drink)

I'm fine. Really. But thanks for worrying. Sorry to ruin your good night's sleep tonight. I love you. Honor bright.

*(*Young Edie *kisses* Sarah *on the cheek and both head upstairs as lights fade out on living room.)*

"EDIE"

I don't remember all the drinking.

EDIE

O.k., now someone make a toast, huh? I think it'll look bad if I toot my own horn.

*(*Charles *looks at* Chip *who may have been about to pounce on a line set-up like that, but refrains.* Chip *signals with a "hands off" gesture.)*

KATE

Have we really time for this, Edie? I am kind of looking forward to hearing that history professor speak and surely Grandmother can't hold our seats forever.

EDIE

No prob. Honestly. First of all, he's into ancient languages and we will all realize quite quickly why Latin is dead. Second of all, you know better than to think that Grandmother couldn't hold down a couple of seats. Nobody will tangle with that feisty old broad, I can assure you . . .

MARIAN

Edith.

EDIE

(Ignoring her mother)

and third of all, it's a five minute walk and we had a rehearsal yesterday. I'm sitting between Buffy Barker and Missy Bernet. So, in answer to your question . . .

CHIP

Finally.

EDIE

. . . yes, we have plenty of time. That is, as long as someone in the next minute makes a toast so we can get on with it.

(She looks significantly at her father.)

CHARLES

Well, I see that although you aren't graduating *summa cum laude* or with a practical degree, it is good . . .

"EDIE"

English.

EDIE

Hey, I'm graduating, aren't I? Nobody said how well I was supposed to do. I did the best I could.

"EDIE"

Didn't I?

*(*Edie *gives* Charles *a look that means he should try again.)*

CHARLES

(Clears his throat)

To Edie, the best in a long line, whose efforts and strengths have combined to . . .

EDIE

Daddy, we don't have that much time and the bubbles are dying. Someone pinch hit please and make it snappy.

JESSIE

(Jumping in)

To Edie. May she have the courage to do what she wants and the strength to be who she is.

(They all toast and drink. Edie *kisses* Jessie. Edie *puts down her cup.* "Edie" *takes the cup and crosses with it into the kitchen.)*

CHARLES

My sentiments exactly. Couldn't have done better myself. Now, Edie, about this prospective job . . .

EDIE

Jessie.

JESSIE

I plead the Fifth.

CHARLES

Edie.

EDIE

Later, Daddy. Another round, anyone?

(She looks around for her cup. When she can't find it, she shrugs and takes a sip from the bottle.)

CHARLES

I think we've had enough.

MARIAN

Yes, perhaps we ought to get going.

EDIE

Party poopers. Jess? Daddy? Chip, surely you . . .

CHARLES

No, Edie, we're through. Let's get going.

EDIE

All right, Daddy. Let's go.

(She begins to exit with the bottle in her hand.)

MARIAN

Edith, where are your shoes?

EDIE

Haven't got them on.

MARIAN

I can see that. Why not?

EDIE

Well,

(Giggles)

I'm not wearing anything else so why should I spoil my ensemble with shoes?

MARIAN AND CHARLES

What?

EDIE

See you afterwards.

(She flips up one leg and dashes out the door before anyone can react.)

MARIAN

Jessie, she's not naked underneath that robe, is she?

*(*Jessie *looks at* Marian *innocently and shrugs his shoulders.)*

CHARLES

Oh, my God. Edith . . .

*(*Charles *chases after her with* Marian *in hot pursuit.)*

MARIAN

Please let my mother never know.

CHIP

What I really don't understand now is, why did it take her so long in the bathroom?

(He grabs a handful of peanuts as Kate, Jessie, *and he exit.)*

"EDIE"

(From the kitchen)

I did everything short of doing a cartwheel on the lawn of the admissions building. Daddy forbade that.

(She crumples the paper cup she took from Edie.*)*

Sometimes I wanted my life to be over with. I think the struggle part or the hard part or maybe the "why" part.

(She crosses into the living room and sits in the rocking chair.)

I was always in such a rush to do it or make it or whatever it was that I was in such a rush to do. I always envisioned myself fifty years from now, already done and then I could relax. All I really wanted to do, I thought, was relax.

(Lights fade to a special on "Edie." *Lights, as if from the hallway, fade up on the downstairs. We hear mellow rock music. As we hear the voices,* "Edie"*'s special fades out.* "Edie" *crosses to her place. Her spot finds her.)*

YOUNG EDIE

No, Janet, that's not the way it is at all. It's not as easy to get around as you think.

JANET

At least you're in the heart of it.

YOUNG EDIE

Fenway Park?

(She turns on the living room lights. Janet *and she have wine glasses in their hands.* Young Edie *is carrying a wine bottle in her other hand.)*

JANET

You don't have to arrange your life around the bus schedule.

YOUNG EDIE

Are you kidding? You have it made. They import the guys for you. Personally selected according to wealth and preppiness.

JANET

Yeah, right. It sounds ideal, but no one told us about the preppy dorks.

*(*Young Edie *looks at her.)*

Oh, yes, they have them. Those are the only ones who sign up to come. It's really depressing. Or we get the rowdy ones. Every year, I swear they account for this in the budget, they expect those goons to knock out several windows and stuff every spring weekend. It's disgusting.

YOUNG EDIE

More wine?

JANET

Uhmmm.

(She takes the last sip and holds out her glass for Young Edie *to refill.)*

YOUNG EDIE

Thank God, my dad buys by the carload lot and he'll never miss a bottle or two . . . a night.

(They both laugh.)

JANET

You're so lucky to have someone already. Especially someone like Jessie. You still have him, don't you?

YOUNG EDIE

Of course. Where's he going to go? Sometimes I can't get rid of him fast enough.

JANET

Still see him a lot then?

YOUNG EDIE

Oh, yeah. All the time. Well, pretty much of the time. We're both supposed to be in school after all.

(She laughs, but Janet *remains concerned.)*

(A kitchen light fades up on the apartment. We hear Edie *offstage. She enters from her bedroom, wearing just a robe.)*

EDIE

One bottle of champagne coming up. You know, that was really great. You were really great. After a little of the bubbly, what say we go for it again? O.k.? Hey, Ron, how about it?

(She crosses slightly offstage and realizes that Ron has fallen asleep.)

You always know how to pick 'em, Edie, old girl.

(She pops the champagne cork and begins to drink from the bottle as the scene downstairs continues.)

JANET

That's great, Edie, really. I'm glad things are still working out.

YOUNG EDIE

Of course they are. Why shouldn't they?

JANET

No reason. Just asking, that's all? Can't a best friend ask?

YOUNG EDIE

Sure.

JANET

I mean, I don't see you so much anymore. We're about to graduate and I just wanted to keep up.

YOUNG EDIE

I know . . . He's seeing someone else, isn't he?

JANET

Huh?

YOUNG EDIE

Don't lie to me, Janet. You know, don't you?

JANET

Edie, I don't know what you're talking about.

YOUNG EDIE

Janet, you've been hinting at it all night. It's not really a new concept to me. So tell me what you know. Please, I need to know.

JANET

Well . . . honestly, Edie, I don't know what . . .

YOUNG EDIE

Janet.

JANET

(Sighs heavily)

He's been seeing someone in my dorm.

(She says this very quickly and in a whisper.)

YOUNG EDIE

Who is she? Do I know her?

JANET

I think you've met her. Remember the weekend you came up? It's . . . it's Sandy.

YOUNG EDIE

Your best friend? My supposed best friend's supposed best friend is sleeping with my boyfriend? How could you let that happen?

JANET

Wait a minute, Edie. I was the last to know about it. Really.

YOUNG EDIE

Not the last, I can assure you.

JANET

Well, I mean at school. They didn't want to tell me.

YOUNG EDIE

I bet. That bastard. I give him everything. What more does he need?

JANET

But you are constantly going out on him.

YOUNG EDIE

Different. Totally different.

JANET

Oh.

"EDIE"

I was fair, if nothing else.

(Upstairs in the apartment, we hear the sound of a key, Edie *and* Jessie *enter.* Edie *and* Young Edie *are wearing the same outfits, to indicate that they are at the same age and approximately the same time in their lives.)*

EDIE

So are you going to tell me about her or what?

"EDIE"

Ah, the double standard. Because as I told Janet . . .

YOUNG EDIE

I mean it doesn't matter to me at all, not really. He can see whom he wants. I just don't want to know about it.

JANET

But you asked me . . .

JESSIE

There's nothing to tell, Edie. I swear.

EDIE AND YOUNG EDIE

Hmmpf.

JESSIE AND JANET

It was just one weekend. What's the big deal?

EDIE

What's the big deal?

YOUNG EDIE

What's the big deal?

EDIE

I'll tell you what's the big deal.

Edie	Young Edie
You hurt me.	He hurt me.

Edie and Young Edie

That's the big deal.

Jessie

Ah, I forgot. We mustn't damage the precious goods.

Edie

You're damn straight, buster. You know what's the worst thing about this? I had to hear about it last week from my best friend who saw you sneaking around. God, I wonder who else knows.

Jessie

Who cares? And besides, who made it Janet's business anyway?

Edie

I did. She's my best friend. Were you ever going to tell me?

Jessie

I don't know. It obviously holds more significance to you than it ever did for me.

Edie

That's not the point and you know it.

Jessie

Here we go again.

Young Edie

I'm much too good for him anyway.

(She finishes the last drop of wine.)

Come on, Janet, let's go over to the Star Cafe and find some action.

Janet

But, Edie . . .

*(*Young Edie *exits.)*

We just left there.

*(*Janet *sighs and exits, following* Young Edie.*)*

(Lights fade out on the living room. The scene continues in the apartment.)

JESSIE

The law of inertia was written about you — once you get going, you can't be stopped, but once you're stopped, you don't budge.

EDIE

Now what in the hell is that supposed to mean? I love it when people are cute and psychoanalyze me.

"EDIE"

"There once was a girl with a curl right in the middle of her forehead. When she was good, she was very, very good, but when she was bad she was horrid."

EDIE

You drive me to drink sometimes.

JESSIE

I hardly think I am the cause of your drinking.

EDIE

Well, someone has to be.

JESSIE

It could be you, you know.

EDIE

(She looks at him hard for a beat.)

I don't think there's ever been any doubt that I am.

(Lights fade out slowly on the apartment. Lights fade up quickly on the living room. Charles *and* Marian *are sitting and sipping.)*

(We hear the sound of the front door being slammed. Young Edie *enters.)*

YOUNG EDIE

Dork.

MARIAN

Can you not find a less colloquial word to use, dear? Surely after all your education . . .

YOUNG EDIE

Right, Mother, got it.

CHARLES

Edith, don't talk to your mother like that.

YOUNG EDIE

Sorry, Daddy. I just don't understand how you can sit here night after night, sipping your scotch . . .

CHARLES

(He lifts his glass as in a toast.)

Martini for me.

YOUNG EDIE

It's the same thing.

CHARLES

Hardly, my dear.

YOUNG EDIE

Whatever . . . and worry about my language or some other insane piddly problem when the rest of the world is falling apart.

CHARLES

Well, that's quite a how-do-you-do.

YOUNG EDIE

I'm serious, Daddy. You and Chip and even Jessie are all alike. What are we doing here with all this, this privilege and when are we going to better mankind, or even ourselves? Huh? Answer me that one. Good evening, by the way.

CHARLES

Thank you.

MARIAN

I believe social consciousness has been aroused in our baby.

YOUNG EDIE

You're damn straight it has.

CHARLES

Edith.

YOUNG EDIE

Sorry, Daddy.

MARIAN

And your sister? Is she not included in our illustrious and degenerate group.

YOUNG EDIE

I'm not sure yet about her. She's on an intellectual plane that almost negates her from a guilt or social category.

(Marian *and* Charles *look at each other.)*

God, even Sarah, Sarah, who comes from it and sees it all the time, is worse than all of us. What's her gig?

CHARLES

Gig?

(Marian *shrugs her shoulders.)*

YOUNG EDIE

Oh, never mind. I knew you wouldn't understand. Sometimes I wonder if it's even worth talking to you after eight o'clock.

(Young Edie *storms upstairs.)*

MARIAN

Well.

CHARLES

Another drink, dear?

MARIAN

Definitely.

(Lights fade out on the living room. The spot remains on "Edie."*)*

"EDIE"

And I always thought I was such a well-behaved child.

(Lights fade up on the apartment.)

JESSIE

I don't know why I did it, Edie. It's really not important, is it?

EDIE

Yes, it is.

(Pause)

Would you like to see other women? Jess? Is that what you want?

JESSIE

No. I don't know why . . . I mean, I guess, I guess I was feeling ignored, or you were in one of your moods, or I was lonely. You've been pretty involved with your work lately and it feels funny when you're not around. I don't know, Edie. It just happened, o.k.?

EDIE

Was it nice?

JESSIE

Huh?

EDIE

Was it nice? I mean, did you have a nice time?

JESSIE

I guess so.

EDIE

More than with me? I mean, did you like being with her more than me?

JESSIE

That's not a fair question.

EDIE

Sure it is.

JESSIE

No, Edie. The difference is that I love you. You can hardly compare the woman I love with a woman I, just, uh, well, you know . . .

EDIE

No, tell me. I really don't know.

JESSIE

Had sex with. Are you happy now?

EDIE

I try so hard, Jess. I really do. I try to be everything you need and want and everything my family wants me to be, but sometimes I just can't be, I guess, and I suppose that's why this all happened. I don't know how to be any better than I am. I don't know how to be good enough.

JESSIE

For who? For me? Or for you? If we have to qualify it, you are "good enough" for me. You are most definitely "good enough" for me. Sometimes it scares me just how good enough you are for me. I'm caught, too, Edie. You don't understand that sometimes. I do know what you're struggling with. Somehow, it's much easier for me to accept. Maybe someday I will sit around with my pipe and martini and swear at the stock reports, but it will be because I came to that kind of life. Because the two of us tried everything else and finally we came back to what we knew, not like an old shoe, but rather as the best way to live our lives the way we can and want to. And maybe that's immature or impulsive to say, but I think that's what love is all about and as far as my affair goes, let's drop it. I'm obviously not completely ready to be as responsible as I want to be. And that's just it.

EDIE

Promise you'll never leave me, Jess. Honor bright.

JESSIE

(Pause)

I promise I'll never leave you. Honor bright.

EDIE

And I promise I'll never leave you.

"EDIE"

Honor bright.

EDIE

I'm happy now.

JESSIE

Phew.

EDIE

I don't think I'll ever know why you let me do that to you. Sometimes, I just wonder.

JESSIE

So do I, Edie. So do I.

*(*Jessie *shakes his head and kisses* Edie *on the forehead. Lights fade out on apartment. The spot remains on* "Edie."*)*

"EDIE"

I always said that life would be easier for everyone concerned if they would only do just as I wanted them to do, whatever it was that I wanted them to do, when I wanted them to do it.

(Snaps her fingers)

(Lights fade up on the living room. Chip *is reading.* Kate *is playing the piano.)*

YOUNG EDIE

(Offstage)

. . . and please, please, Sarah, will you make your world-famous, most delicious strawberry-blueberry shortcake for dessert?

SARAH

(Offstage)

I don't know, Edie. Both of those fruits are hard to find now without costing a fortune.

YOUNG EDIE

Oh, please, Sarah. It would mean so much to me. You know, like the Last Supper.

SARAH

Lord, Edie, don't be so morbid. You're just going off to college. It's not that bad.

*(*Young Edie *and* Sarah *enter from kitchen.* Sarah *is carrying sheets.)*

YOUNG EDIE

It may be for me. So, what do you say? You wouldn't deny a condemned woman her last request, would you?

CHIP

How about a cigarette? That's easier, eh, Sarah?

SARAH

Oh, Edie, it'll take so much time to make the biscuits and the whipped cream and get to the store . . .

YOUNG EDIE

(She gets down on her knees and bats her eyes.)

Please, I'm begging now. How can you resist these big brown eyes?

SARAH

Oh, for God's sake, Edie. Sometimes I wonder about you. All right, anything for you tonight, but that's it — absolutely the last request.

YOUNG EDIE

(She hugs Sarah.*)*

Oh, Sarah, you're a doll. I wonder if I can hide you at college. What will I do without you?

SARAH

Get yourself into a ton of trouble, no doubt.

(She exits upstairs.)

YOUNG EDIE

(Enters into the living room)

So, have you heard the good news?

CHIP

If you are referring to your recent triumph over Sarah regarding dessert, one could hardly help overhearing.

YOUNG EDIE

No, dope. Mom and Dad are letting me have an apartment so I don't have to stay in the dorm.

KATE

(Stops playing)

I don't think that's a very good idea.

YOUNG EDIE

I do. Have you seen those cement block things they call housing?

KATE

Well, that's not exactly what I meant. I think it can be a very rewarding experience to meet new friends and share with them. Particularly in your first year. There is so much to learn and see and do.

YOUNG EDIE

Look, Katie, I know all that stuff already. Don't forget we went to a very prestigious college preparatory school. I already know that I am at least two years ahead of most of my future classmates.

CHIP

And God forbid we should mix, is that it, Edie?

YOUNG EDIE

Well, I don't mean to sound like some kind of snob, but, well, I don't know. I thought it would be fun to have a place of my own.

KATE

There's plenty of time for that when you get older.

YOUNG EDIE

When are you going to get older, Kate?

(Silence)

(Lights fade up on apartment. Edie *and* Janet *are hanging out.)*

JANET

God, Edie, you are so lucky to have a place of your own.

EDIE

It does have its advantages. It hasn't always been a bed of roses, though.

Young Edie

I'm sorry, Katie. You know me. Sometimes, I just say the stupidest things without thinking. And then, it's too late to take them back. That's me — Miss Impulsive.

Kate

It's o.k., Edie. You're right, partly. But we just see things differently, you and I. I think I'll go see if Sarah needs a hand with dinner. If you will both excuse me.

(She exits upstairs.)

Chip

You pill brain. When are you going to wise up?

Young Edie

Hey, I said I was sorry. I can't help it. I'm not as smart as you are.

Chip

Oh, you're plenty smart enough. You just don't know when to use it.

Young Edie

Well, I was only speaking the truth.

Chip

Sometimes it pays to be a little less truthful, dear sister. That's just not good enough, Edie.

*(*Chip *exits.)*

"Edie"

I never realized . . .

Young Edie

Shit.

(Lights fade out on the living room. The scene continues in the apartment.)

Edie

Hey, you remember the time we decided to throw eggs at the English department's windows. When was that?

JANET

Summer after our freshman year, I think. God, you were still so mad at them.

EDIE

I remember that you wouldn't throw any. Why not?

JANET

I don't know.

EDIE

Did you think it was a dumb thing to do?

JANET

No, I don't remember thinking about it one way or the other. I just knew I wasn't that mad to do something like that.

"EDIE"

(Snaps her fingers)

Edith, your utopia wasn't good enough.

(Snaps her fingers again)

JANET

So, how's the job?

EDIE

O.k., I guess. They keep wanting to add more hours. I get a little tired of dunking film in solution all day. It's not exactly the photography career I had in mind.

JANET

Well, what did you expect? It's a photography lab, for God's sake, and you're not a junior cub reporter for *Life* magazine. Sometimes you expect too much too soon.

"EDIE"

Why can't I have that?

EDIE

I suppose so. Have you seen my latest shots? There is one advantage to this job — I can develop my own stuff for free.

(She brings out a package which contains some eight-by-ten black-and-white photographs.)

JANET

(Looking through them)

My God, Edie, these are really good. Where did you take them?

EDIE

Oh, Jessie and I went up to Maine a couple of weekends ago. I seem to be in some kind of "nature" period. My boss saw them and said I should enter them for this contest coming up.

JANET

Are you going to? They really are very good. I mean, I don't claim to be any judge or anything.

EDIE

Yeah, I think I will.

JANET

You know, you could probably take some great shots up at Chippewa this summer.

EDIE

Oh, yeah, I could, I guess.

JANET

I'm really looking forward to this summer. Aren't you?

EDIE

Uhm, yeah, I am.

JANET

Edie, I don't like your tone. We are going back to Chippewa, aren't we? We always go. We've been going together since we were eleven. I was counting on it. We've been there so long, I'm surprised they haven't named a cabin or two after us.

EDIE

Yeah, well, that was exactly my thinking, Janet. I mean, we've done that already. Maybe too much. Now it's time to do something new.

JANET

Edie. What do you have in mind?

EDIE

Uh, actually, Jessie and I were discussing doing something together, like taking his Jeep and going cross country for awhile. Camp out, see the country, things like that.

JANET

Oh, I see.

EDIE

Well, I thought all three of us could go. We would split everything three ways. It would be a lot of laughs.

JANET

Yeah.

EDIE

You don't like that idea?

JANET

Oh, no, Edie, it's a great idea. It's just that it comes as quite a shock, you know, all of a sudden like. I was expecting one thing and now it's completely something else. I had planned to earn some money this summer since I am going to Europe in the fall. I mean, summer camp counselor isn't on the list for jobs in which you do make money, but my folks thought it would be all right. I don't know about this other thing, though, Edie.

EDIE

I only said it was a thought. God, Janet, it's not like we've decided everything already. I still have to tell my parents.

JANET

I suppose.

EDIE

Don't be bummed. Things will work out. Let's just wait and see. So, have you got your trip all planned out? I can't believe that you are going to Europe for six months. Some lucky break, having an aunt who lives in Paris.

JANET

Well, we've decided that I'm going to use Paris as our base and then take side trips wherever we want to go. I mean, I've barely got my passport, but she said we could go anywhere.

EDIE

Six months. What a great graduation present. I'm going to miss you.

JANET

That's why I thought this summer would be so much fun. Just the two of us, like old times.

EDIE

You're right. I hadn't thought about it like that.

"EDIE"

Ouch.

EDIE

Well, let's not get morbid yet. How about a beer?

(As Edie *crosses to the kitchen, the lights fade out on the apartment. Lights fade up on the living room.* Young Edie *is on the phone.)*

YOUNG EDIE

Janet? ... What's up? ... What are you doing? ... You're watching public television? ... Are you serious? I'm coming over there and rescuing you. You need help ... Come on, it's our last night of freedom. Let's get into trouble ... It'll be fun. Besides, they always rerun those programs on Wednesday night anyway ...

(Laughs)

Right. See you in a bit.

*(*Young Edie *hangs up, grabs a jacket and some car keys, and skips out the front door. Lights on the living room fade out. The spot remains on* "Edie."*)*

"Edie"

I had this recurring dream as a child. Growing up in the Midwest, we'd get these great electrical thunderstorms. They're really beautiful. We'd turn off all the lights, light some candles and huddle around in the living room listening to the rain pelt on the roof and watch the world come to an end. Sometimes it felt like that. The whole sky would light up, with this eerie blue light and everyone was exposed for that brief flash, almost like a strobe, frozen in time for a second. God, it was great. Thunderstorms meant spring and spring also meant tornados. These I was never fond of. The minute I heard the weather bulletin, I'd head for the northeast corner of our basement. I was always sure it would hit this time. My parents thought I was a little strange, but I didn't care. I was going to be safe. But then, I'd have this dream. We live at the end of a lane. I see the tornado coming down the lane. It's not a very wide one because it is staying on the street and only taking out a few mailboxes and trees. But I see that it's heading for our house. I begin walking toward it. It's coming toward me and we meet, right at the base of the property. It stands still, right there in front of me, still twirling and swishing, but I remain calm. I'm carrying some pots and pans because there is an old Indian superstition that if you can confuse the tornado, or scare it, it'll go away, and all I really want to do is stop it before it hurts my family. And so we have a little chat, the tornado and me. I tell it I want it to leave, go back, leave us alone. I bang the pots a bit, threaten to throw them in, and the tornado looks at me. It listens, I bang my pots again, and it looks at me for a good long minute. And then, the most incredible thing happens — it leaves. It shrivels up or sometimes it just rises back into the sky, but it leaves. When I asked it, it always went away.

(The spot goes to black. We hear voices in the dark living room.)

Charles

This is ridiculous.

MARIAN

Charles.

CHARLES

I mean it, Marian. How long have we been waiting?

CHIP

Only since before the fall of Rome.

MARIAN

Chip, dear, please.

*(*Charles *lights a match.)*

MARIAN

Put out that light, Charles. She's due any minute.

CHARLES

I'm sorry, but this is not my idea of a surprise birthday party. Four people.

SARAH

(Enters)

Don't forget about me.

CHARLES

Ouch.

(The match has burned down and burned his fingers.)

Yes, of course, Sarah. But, seriously, Marian, this really doesn't cut the cake, as it were. Where are all her supposed best friends?

MARIAN

It's not like when she was in high school. They're all off doing other things, living in other places.

CHIP

Everyone who is anyone has flown the coop.

CHARLES

Meaning . . . ?

Chip

Nothing obvious, sir.

Kate

What about Janet, though? She is coming, isn't she?

Marian

It depends. She was going to leave for Florida right after her job interview today. But she may make it.

Charles

Her own best friend. This is going to be a fine celebration.

Marian

It will be, Charles. Even if it is just the family, I'm sure she'll appreciate it.

Kate

I hope so. Having those photographs rejected hit her pretty hard.

Chip

Well, what does she expect? Criminy, it was the first time she ever submitted them.

"Edie"

Right.

Charles

Well, no matter for the moment. Your mother's right. We need to show Edie a good time. Jessie will be here, won't he?

Marian

Of course, dear, he's playing confederate for us. They are having drinks together and I made him promise to have her here by eight.

Charles

And what time is it now?

Sarah

Eight-fifteen.

CHARLES

Have you got eyes that glow in the dark, Sarah?

SARAH

No. My digital watch has a light thing in it.

CHARLES

Speaking of lights, I'm turning them on. This is stupid, Marian.

EVERYONE

No.

MARIAN

Majority rules, dear.

CHARLES

Only when it's in your favor.

(He heads for what he thinks is the bar and runs into Kate *at the piano.)*

KATE

Hello, Father. It's me.

CHARLES

Sorry, Kate.

MARIAN

Charles, what are you doing now?

CHARLES

I'm trying to find the bar. At least if you insist I sit in the dark, let me be smashed in the dark.

(He crashes into something else.)

Blast.

SARAH

(She has managed to cross to the bar and mix a martini for Charles *and hands it to him.)*

Here, sir.

CHARLES

You were a cat in your former life, Sarah, I swear.

SARAH

No, I've just been working here too long. I could find my way blindfolded and spun around twenty times.

CHARLES

Meaning . . . ?

SARAH

Nothing obvious, sir.

(They all laugh.)

CHARLES

This is beginning to have a more festive atmosphere. Drinks, anyone? Sarah, would you mind . . . ? Now, if I could only find my place again.

MARIAN

Perhaps you are better off right where you are for the moment. She should be here any time now.

CHARLES

Maybe we could get one of those little bathroom light things. You know, those night things, just for the glow.

CHIP

That would be great. Mickey Mouse in the Barnett living room.

MARIAN

Really, dear, be patient. Just a little while longer.

(The front door opens. Edie *and* Jessie *enter.* Sarah *swiftly crosses to the foyer and switches on the lights.)*

SARAH

Surprise, baby.

(As the lights come up on the living room, they also come up on the apartment. Young Edie *is startled.* Charles, Marian, Kate, *and* Chip *are slightly confused about what to do.)*

EVERYONE

Happy birthday, Edie.

EDIE

Oh, no.

JESSIE

Edie, damn it . . .

*(*Edie *rushes up the stairs.* Jessie *starts to follow. He looks at the family and indicates that they will be down in a minute. Several beats of more confusion follow. Then* Jessie *comes halfway down the stairs.)*

JESSIE

Kate.

(He goes back up the stairs. Kate *takes her position at the piano, beginning a "drum roll."* Edie *and* Jessie *descend the stairs.)*

"EDIE"

This isn't right, I want you to know.

EDIE

(Sotto voce)

What's going on here, Jessie?

JESSIE

Act surprised, pumpkin . . .

(She shoots him a look.)

and touched.

EDIE

Oh, that's the key, here, eh?

JESSIE

Yes, ma'am.

*(*Kate *is about to launch into "Happy Birthday" on the piano, but* Jessie *cuts her off.)*

MARIAN

Happy birthday, baby.

*(*Marian *crosses to* Edie. *She hugs and kisses her.* Edie *receives this as well as she can.)*

EDIE

Thanks, Mother.

KATE

Happy birthday, Edie.

*(*Kate *hugs and kisses* Edie.*)*

CHIP

Ditto, Sis.

EDIE

Thanks, Bro.

(Finally, Charles *gets his act together, for, in the confusion, he managed to spill his drink.)*

CHARLES

Ah, herself has arrived. Happy birthday, darling.

*(*Charles *kisses and hugs* Edie.*)*

EDIE

Thank you, Daddy. I'm quite . . . touched.

(She looks at Jessie *as if to say, "Was that all right?" He indicates that it was.)*

CHARLES

And Jessie, glad to see you could make it.

EDIE

(To Jessie*)*

Did you have a choice?

*(*Jessie *smiles and shakes his head, "Not really." They both laugh.* Edie *is beginning to cheer up.)*

EDIE

So, where are the gifts? And the champagne? And the dancing girls? This is a birthday party, correct?

CHARLES

(Surprised, yet delighted by the change in Edie.*)*

Of course. Sarah . . . ?

*(*Sarah *has already popped the cork on the champagne bottle and begins pouring and distributing glasses.)*

EDIE

God, I hope you didn't get a cake. I was just embarrassed by my so-called friend here. A candle in a cupcake. That's charming, isn't it?

KATE

I think it's kind of romantic.

EDIE

Actually, it was.

(She kisses Jessie.*)*

He's o.k., I guess. I think I'll keep him around for awhile.

JESSIE

Do I have a choice?

*(*Edie *shakes her head "not really." They both laugh.)*

(The doorbell rings.)

CHARLES

(Mock surprise)

My goodness, I wonder who that could be?

EDIE

Are we expecting other trick or treaters?

*(*Jessie *crosses to the front door to answer it.)*

JESSIE

(Offstage)

I was hoping it was you.

JANET

(Offstage)

It wasn't easy to rearrange my schedule but . . .

EDIE

Janet? How wonderful.

*(*Edie *begins to cross to the foyer to greet her friend, as* Jessie *and* Janet *enter.* Janet *sports an attractive business suit, pumps, blouse with a big bow. Her hair is neatly coiffed, she has on makeup and carries a briefcase and a wrapped gift.)*

EDIE

Oh, my God.

"EDIE"

What has she done?

JANET

Happy twenty-third, baby.

"EDIE"

Baby?

JANET

Well, aren't you at least glad to see me? It has, after all, been a long time.

"EDIE"

I should say so.

EDIE

Of course, silly.

*(*Edie *hugs and kisses* Janet.*)*

But where, in God's name, did you get those clothes?

JANET

I had a job interview today. Account executive. You know, usual stuff.

EDIE

It's not usual for me.

JANET

It will be. Good evening, Mr. Barnett, Mrs. Barnett. Hello, Kate. So nice to see you again.

(She goes about the room, shaking hands, greeting people, very formally.)

Sarah . . . ? Where . . . ?

SARAH

I'll take it.

*(*Sarah *takes the present from* Janet *and puts it on the piano.)*

JANET

(To Chip*)*

Thanks again for last night. I sure had a great time.

"EDIE"

What?

JANET

I'm sorry I'm late. I guess I missed the big surprise.

"EDIE"	EDIE
Oh, no, she didn't.	Oh, no, you didn't.

MARIAN

We're glad to see you could make it, dear.

JANET

Well, I changed my plane reservations for tomorrow morning. I lost out on the super-saver deal, but, hey, this seemed worth it.

EDIE

Where are you going?

JANET

Florida. I'm meeting my parents in Sarasota to help them set up house. They just bought this beautiful condo on the beach and Dad even bought a sailboat. Could you die? My father? He's so into it. Of course, the first sign of barnacles, the thing is going up for sale. But it's fun for them right now.

CHIP

I can imagine.

EDIE

Jessie . . .

JESSIE

(Brushes her off)

That sounds like fun, Janet.

JANET

Yes, I suppose so.

CHARLES

Well, Janet, tell us homebodies your thoughts from abroad. That must have been some experience.

JANET

It was a lot of little experiences. But I don't want to bore you with all those details. Surely my mother has been keeping you up on it.

MARIAN

Of course, dear. It certainly sounded exciting.

JANET

Oh, it was. I must say, I surprised myself with my French. I was speaking like a native in no time. I wish Edie could have come over at Christmas like we planned. We would have had a great time, Edie.

EDIE

I'm sure.

"EDIE"

I was all set to go visit Janet. Why didn't I?

KATE

What are your plans after Florida? Will you be coming back here and settling down for awhile?

JANET

Well, I guess it all depends a lot on the job market. Mother and Father would like me to move with them to Florida, but we'll see. I mean, I've been gone almost a year and a half. I still haven't quite adjusted.

CHARLES

Just what exactly are you looking for?

JANET

Oh, you know, a corporate middle management entry level position.

*(*Edie *rolls her eyes.)*

Just like everybody else, I suppose.

EDIE

But, Janet you were an art history major. What business is going to hire you to manage them?

JANET

Well, I did minor in economics.

"EDIE"

You did? I don't remember that.

*(*Edie *looks surprised at Janet's remark and then begins to pace.)*

JANET

I wasn't exactly a stellar student, Edie. I majored in art history because it was fun. It sure did pay off this past year in Europe, though. But, as far as using that to get a practical or profitable job, it doesn't seem to be there, at least not for me.

EDIE

Huh.

CHARLES

Well, that all sounds exciting. Best of luck to you, Janet.

JANET

Thank you, Mr. Barnett.

EDIE

Jessie . . .

JANET

Would you listen to me babbling on. It's your day, Edie. Tell me all about what's been happening to you.

EDIE

That's easy — nothing.

JANET

Oh, come on. I figured you must be pretty busy since I hardly heard from you.

EDIE

Oh, yeah, sorry about that.

JANET

Well, what about the photography? How's that going?

EDIE

Oh . . . you know . . .

"EDIE"

I wanted to have an exhibition someday. I had started to take classes . . .

JESSIE

She's been taking classes and from all accounts, her teachers are very impressed with her work.

EDIE

Yeah, I have limited scope, but what I shoot, I shoot well. Whatever that means.

JESSIE

It means that she sees things like no one else does. That's what makes her good.

EDIE

That's not true, Jessie.

JESSIE

Of course it is. That's what your teacher said. Didn't he?

EDIE

Yes.

JANET

Well, I trust you are pursuing it. How's the job at the lab?

(Everyone *looks at* Edie.)

EDIE

Oh, well, I got tired of that. I'm trying my hand at freelancing — you know, weddings, portraits. Actually, mostly baby pictures and street stuff.

"EDIE"

It's true. I was pretty good. But . . .

EDIE

Jessie . . .

JESSIE

Cut it out.

MARIAN

(Watching Edie's *restlessness)*

Edith, please calm down. Relax. It's your birthday. Is something wrong?

EDIE

Uh, no, I'm fine.

JANET

So, Kate, what's been going on with you? Still teaching at Chatham?

KATE

Yes.

CHARLES

And doing a fine job.

KATE

Dad.

CHARLES

Well, you are.

EDIE

(To Jessie*)*

Can we go?

JESSIE

(To Edie*)*

We don't have anywhere to go, Edie. Come on, let's have some fun.

EDIE

Yeah.

*(*Edie *continues to pace as lights downstairs begin to fade. Lights remain on* "Edie."*)*

"EDIE"

That was the beginning of the end, I guess. Jessie and I went back to Boston — he to finish his fall term, and I — well, I plunged feverishly into my photography. It seemed my only salvation at the time. I thought I was still doing good work. As for Janet, I'm not sure just what happened. I suppose my mother tried to keep me posted, but I really don't remember any of the details. I tried to see someone professionally because I was having trouble focusing. I remember coming home for that Christmas. But everything was the same. Chip had joined the law firm and Kate was still teaching. And my mother and father, well, they were still my mother and father. But something wasn't right. I kept hoping it would pass, but, too many things kept crossing my path. One by one, I felt my options had slipped by, and that's when I decided to do it.

(Throughout the rest of the play, the lights will isolate these exchanges.)

JESSIE

Cut it out, Edie. I'm tired of hearing about it. You won't let me help you.

EDIE

I don't know how to ask for it.

JESSIE

Call me when you're out of this mood.

YOUNG EDIE

It just happens, Jess. I can control it.

JESSIE

That's not good enough. I'm history, Edie.

EDIE AND YOUNG EDIE

No.

"EDIE"

Wait a minute. That didn't happen . . . did it?

CHIP

Take it from a pro. It's not that hard. Relax.

EDIE AND YOUNG EDIE

Yeah, relax. That's it.

"EDIE"

No, don't. You can't.

YOUNG EDIE

I just want to have fun.

EDIE

I just want to be happy.

EDIE AND YOUNG EDIE

Everyone just leave me alone.

JANET

Have you no goals at all, Edie?

EDIE

You know what I want to do. I want to go to the Orient. You know, sit in the Raffles Hotel, drink Singapore slings with this gorgeous Panama hat on, and be a charming dilettante.

JANET

Oh, Edie, that's not what I mean.

"EDIE"

What am I talking about?

KATE

You never did understand moderation, did you? Always black and white.

"EDIE"

Gin?

(All three Edies *snap their fingers.)*

EDIE

Where are the bastards when I need them?

(She gets out a bottle of pills and with a glass of vodka, she swallows a handful. She then begins to pace.)

"EDIE"

Is that how it ends?

EDIE

I want it to stop.

(She begins to snap her fingers uncontrollably.)

"EDIE"

Why now?

YOUNG EDIE

I don't know.

EDIE

All I want to do is relax.

YOUNG EDIE AND "EDIE"

No.

MARIAN

Edie, please get a grip.

YOUNG EDIE

I'm fine, Mother.

"EDIE"

Honor bright.

(She snaps her fingers.)

KATE

She's confused the issues.

YOUNG EDIE

No, I haven't.

"EDIE"

It was my choice. I'm sure it was.

CHIP

It's all a matter of priorities, Edie.

*(*Edie *begins to bang pots and pans together. She will continue this action until the end.)*

EDIE

I'm falling.

"EDIE"

I don't remember any of this.

YOUNG EDIE

Sarah, do you understand the blues?

SARAH

Of course, child.

YOUNG EDIE

Me, too.

*(*Sarah *shakes her head.)*

"EDIE"

No, everybody, stop it. Just stop it. I'm confused. That's not the way it was.

EDIE

I feel so pulled. Why?

JESSIE

It's always gone away before. Don't worry. I understand.

"Edie"

No, you don't. You left me.

Charles

Edie, relax.

"Edie"

No, don't.

Edie

I can't. I don't know how.

Young Edie

Go away. I want you all to go away.

"Edie"

(To Edie*)*

I don't want you to hurt my family.

Kate

Sometimes we don't know what you want from us.

"Edie"

(To Edie*)*

They knew. Hold on.

Janet

You always have before.

Chip

Relax.

Edie

O.k.

"Edie"

No. It was the act of a rational . . .

Marian

(Overlaps)

What's wrong, Edith? You're acting so strange

SARAH

Baby . . . ?

EDIE

Sarah . . . ?

"EDIE"

Oh, my God, what's happening.

EDIE

(Stops banging her pots and pans as she has gotten increasingly drowsy and the last few attempts were misses.)

I'm calm now. It's all right now.

"EDIE"

Nooo.

(Drawn out, in a moan)

YOUNG EDIE

(Clamps her hands over her ears)

Stop it. All of you. Leave me alone.

(Both Young Edie *and* Edie *snap their fingers on both hands. With that,* "Edie" *fades out her moan. There is a blackout, except for spots on the three* Edies.*)*

ALL THREE EDIES

Oh, my God.

(Total blackout)

(As the lights begin a slow fade up, we see the apartment is empty. In the living room, Marian *and* Charles *are sitting and sipping, as in the opening tableau. We hear a pounding on the upstairs door.)*

JESSIE

Edie? Edie? I know you're in there . . . Edieee.

(On his scream, the lights fade out on the apartment.)

(She is still visibly and physically shaken from what she has just seen. She tries to gain composure, takes a minute, and then faces the audience. Another beat. She tries to speak, but realizes that her "planned" speech is not going to work now. She bites her bottom lip. She smiles ironically and slightly shakes her head. She surveys the entire audience for a moment. Then she speaks.)

I . . . I . . . It was rational, wasn't it? . . . It was . . .

(Again, she looks at them as if to speak, but there is nothing more to say or explain. She takes a deep breath, lets it out slowly, and looks away for a moment. Then she looks back at the audience. A half smile.)

Wasn't it?

(Her spot fades to black.)

(End of Act Two.*)*

About the Author

Lue Morgan Douthit holds a master of fine arts degree in playwrighting and directing from Trinity University, which she obtained while apprenticing at the Dallas Theater Center. *Honor Bright* was her master of arts thesis. She currently lives in Los Angeles and is working on an original screenplay and restructuring one of her plays, *And What's To Become of Stanley?*, into a teleplay. Before that she lived in New York City for three and a half years; there she stage-managed and directed Off-Broadway and saw *Honor Bright* produced at the McGinn/Cazale Theatre. Her other credits include being production stage manager for Fort Worth's Shakespeare in the Park and assistant to the literary manager for new plays at the Dallas Theater Center. She has been a playreader for both the Women's Project of the American Place Theatre in New York City and the Arizona Theatre Company. She is a member of The Dramatists Guild and Actor's Equity Association.

Colophon

Honor Bright has been printed in an edition
of five hundred copies on Mohawk Superfine paper
by V. John Sukys, Richard E. Kraft, and Julius P. Sukys
on a Miehle vertical press, Series 50 (text)
and a Heidelberg 10″x15″ platen press (label).
The type, ten-point Bodoni Bold,
has been set by Robert M. Starkman
of the Superior Linotype Company of Cleveland, Ohio.
It has been bound by the Forest City Bindery of Cleveland, Ohio.